IN THE NAME OF LIFE

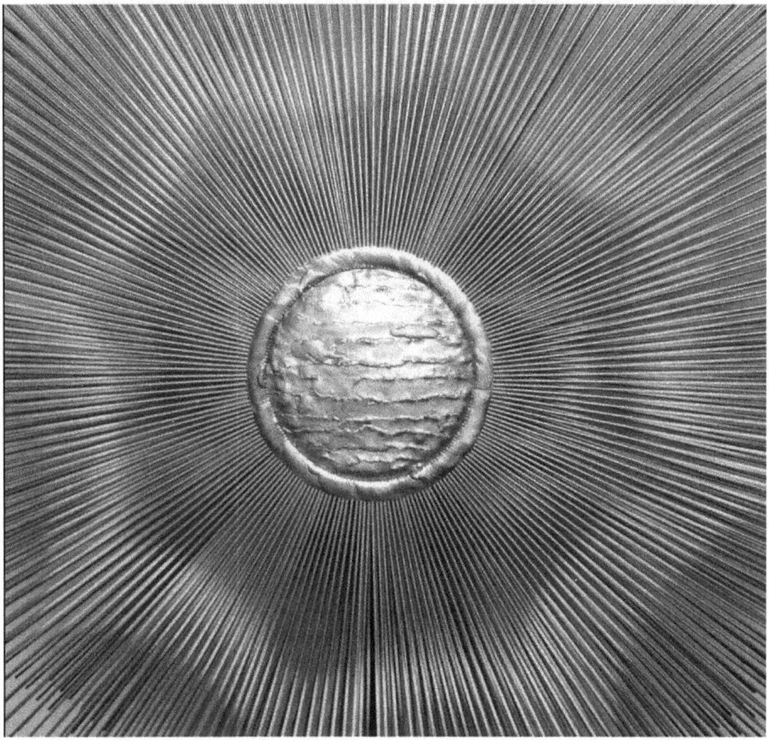

THOMAS S. KAKOVITCH

Copyright © 2018 by Thomas Kakovitch

All rights reserved. Any reproduction in any media without written permission of the publisher is a violation of international copyright law.

Published by: HRD Press, Inc.
22 Amherst Road
Amherst, MA 01002
800-822-2801 (U.S. and Canada)
413-253-3488
413-253-3490 (fax)

ISBN 978-1-61014-427-8

Table of Contents

Preface v
Historical Facts 1
    Turkey 3
    Persia 13
Prelude to World War II 27
    Russia 39
Exile 37
    Siberia 39
Immigration 49
    Iran 51
Europe 65
    France 67
United States of America 73
    Washington, D.C. 75
    Maine 77
    Maryland 79
    Assassination 85
    Further Education 89
Jobs 91
    Washington Technical Institute 93
    University of the District of Columbia 95
    Visitation 97
Internal Affairs 99
    Krakow, Poland 101
    Geopolitical Entrapment 109
Isolation 113
    Grand Canyon 115
    Inspiration 117
    Philosophy and Science 121
    Zone Interdit 127
    Think Tank 129

In the Name of Life

Information 131
Married with Children 133
Innovative Discoveries 137
Royal Family 139
Life and Family 143
Incomprehensible 145
September 11, 2001 147
Culture 151
Joy and Sadness 153
Vigilance 155
Out-of-the-Box Thinking 157
Final Stage 161

Preface

This is why science always wins—because we are beaten by its facts.

What could be simpler than light? All that we observe emits light. We studied it and discovered that it consists of photons. What is a photon? Photon is nature's energy delivery truck. Our sun emits plenty of photons. Where are these solar photons coming from? From its raging interior; its core. Solar photons are forged by the fusion of four hydrogen atoms to form helium. These are the first and second elements present in nature. How is it that every star in the universe is able to ignite a fusion? Because it is the law. The star's gravity will produce the high pressures and temperatures required to ignite a fusion. If photons are truck-like entities that deliver energy, how fast can they move in empty space? With the speed of light. Photons are not trucks, they are actually radiations and are smaller than atoms. All solar photons start as gamma radiation in the core of the sun. They journey toward the surface of the sun. This journey takes hundreds of thousands of years. The gamma rays must traverse the deep solar plasma zone. As these gamma rays ascend to the surface, they lose energy and transform into much longer waves, part of which is visible light. The upward ascent toward the surface is not "measured" in time, but in temperature. And "measurement" is not a quality, but a quantity. The ascent of the gamma rays follows the principles of quantification. Studying something as simple as light turns out to be a field of study based on the principles of quantification, or quantum. To understand light, we must "measure" it and quantify it. "Let there be light" may be a philosophy, a qualitative description of an event; however, can it be asked whether or not "measurement," or quantification, may also be nature's request from life? Why?

Life is science. Life is a dialogue between all that is nature. What ingredient is added to a carbon chain molecule that can turn a polymer into a conversational being? We can take organic molecules such as milk, sugar, butter, or grain, mix them together, and even add some heat to the mixture. We may get a cookie but not necessarily life, especially one that is constantly in communication with its contour.

We live and die, that is a fact. The appearance of a few facts may not necessarily be sufficient to claim some sort of natural coherence. There is always the danger of transforming just a few events into something more than they really are. It is a bad statistic to reach a conclusion based only on a few samples. To turn faith into a beautifully narrated poetry is one thing, but to scientifically show that life is nothing more than the fusion of earthly sperms and eggs is a different story.

Consider the case of an earthly rover on the Martian landscape in a remote dialogue with some stations on a far and different planet. What if by some miracle one day the rover asked itself an innocent question. "With whom am I communicating?" Could such behavior describe the beginning of spiritualism? We gave the rover a reason to be, not that it necessarily wanted one, but communication flew through it non-stop and it could not comprehend that the dialogue was not of it, nor was it of Mars.

Not all things in life are what they seem to be. Not all stories, even in the Bible, are what they are dialogued. Moses was a good general, but not a magician who could part the waters of the Red Sea. He could have used his wargame analysis to know how to neutralize Ramses' advantageous armament, namely, the chariots. He would have to choose a battleground where chariots were no longer an asset, but rather a total liability. A swap would do, the "reed" sea. Years later a simple narrative in a different version mutated part of a history into a religion. Even thousands of years later, one such mutation turned cousins against each other.

The dialogue among mankind is short, but the communication between humans and "God" is long. Imagine us to be highly complex carbonic rovers on earth with the capacity to differentiate between spiritualism and an uncontrolled chaos. Imagine if we were not "know it all," but accepted our limitations about the knowledge of how all of nature, from the elementary particles to the cosmos, is orchestrated and harmonized in the midst of works of chaos. We could have deduced that nature shows no preference. It does not have a preference for which hydrogen atoms make which stars, and which stars should make which galaxies. Whatever forges a stability and follows the rules of gravitational attraction will do.

Imagine with all the Nobel laurates in economy if someone had told the Cod fisherman in Iceland that organizing banking finance is not truly a science yet, that we do not understand it and much less predict it, and that Iceland is still a nation and not a "hedge fund." Iceland, for humanity's sake, don't amass a debt equivalent to 850 percent of your GDP.

We know somehow in the pure vacuum of space elementary particles appear and disappear by means of fluctuating energy. Information is transmitted, captured and transformed. Which information has priority, and why? If all the rock on Mars transmitted information, we would only concern ourselves with what our rover is transmitting. No other radiation in the form of the electromagnetic waves would appear to be as important. Why, one should ask? Because we created the rover, soft landed it on Mars, and exchanged information between mankind and a machine on another planet. Why is that important? It is important only to us. We prioritized it. What for? To give ourselves a reason for existing.

If we were to interfere with an extended reasoning and this time assume that we were a kind of biological machine on earth, where communication flew through us non-stop, and where a dialogue was neither of us nor of Earth, what would possess our creator to prophesize into the future that he, she, or it also existed once?

HISTORICAL FACTS

Turkey

Mountaineers

Not all that I am is known to me. But I know I came to exist because of what was there before me. Somehow, I seemed to have lived several lives in one.

During the Great War—which great war? There have been so many. The First World War (1914 to 1918) was another tragedy in the annals of tragedies. All of those who have lost loved ones are victims. In any conflict, loved ones die. Victims are the total sum of all that are involved in killings or being killed. No race, religion, or creed is saved from becoming a victim. It is usually a matter of time who will turn against whom. It may not even be as simple as different ideologies or politics, or even the fall of economies, but rather an overall desperation that consumes all, even those who started the destruction in the first place. It is almost irrelevant who was at fault, whether it was Romanov, Habsburg, or Kaiser Wilhelm, at the end they too vanished. Inertia, by definition, is the resistance to change of direction during a motion. Wars, or mass killings in general, seem to follow the principle of inertia. Once they are in motion, they are resistant to a change of direction until it is too late. Collateral damages, as they are known, do not come close to describing the pain that will last for generations. The victims feel guilty. As strange as it may sound, but that is the truth. They feel as if they have done something wrong. Why else would anyone want to destroy them? This is where faith and reason entangle in a dance macabre. Some may be able to disengage themselves from a downward spin and choose either faith or reason as an outlet. For others, sorrow will be their companion till the end.

The beginning of the war in August of 1914 pushed the Assyrian mountaineers into a period of absolute isolation. Mar Shimun was the Assyrian Patriarch. The dark clouds of the massacre of Christians were forming. The Armenian massacre was reported from all sides.

In the Name of Life

Fighting was reported on the Turko-Persian borders, in the Assyrian districts of Tergawar and Margawar, between the local Christians and the Begzade Kurds of the region. At the beginning of November, Turkey entered the war on the side of Germany. License was issued to the Kurds to sack the Christian village of Albaq, near Bashkala, under the eyes of the Ottoman local authority. This was the case, even though there was a disposition in many Kurds to recognize the Patriarch of their Christian neighborhood as the possessor of a sort of honorary religious precedent in all Kurdistan.

The first fighting took place in Persia, which the Turks at that time determined to regard as a Russian province. Regular Ottoman troops and Kurdish irregulars swept over the border, drove the Christians from Tergawar, and came down toward Urmia, intending to occupy the region and call on the Shiah Mussalman population to forget all feuds in Islam, and join them in the Jihad which had already been proclaimed. The Russian troops in Urmia, which formed the consular guard, had stored a considerable number of rifles. These rifles were issued to the men of Tergawar which formed two battalions under the supervision of Russian officers. Even though the men of Tergawar fought well, the odds were against them. The invaders pushed on toward Charbash, a Christian village barely a mile away from the obsolete mud walls of the town of Urmia. The Muslims were in absolute confidence of victory, so much so that the Kurdish irregulars threw away their reserves of bread, having been told by their superiors, "you will not need stale bread, you will be eating fresh bread in Urmia tomorrow." The well-timed arrival of Russian reinforcements saved the situation. The Kurdish attack proved to be a costly failure, and the Kurds were glad to get back to their hills before the winter set in before the Christmas of 1914, which in the Eastern world, falls thirteen days later than in the West.

For a while, Urmia considered itself to be saved, particularly when the Russian column went down south to Saj Bulak to inflict a severe defeat upon a second Kurdish force at Dol. Another district was cleared. The American missionaries had come to the Urmia region to help the Christians. The Russian officers were uneasy about the situation in the Caucasus, and would not pledge themselves to a permanent occupation, having told the American missionaries that they would, however, give them ample warning to evacuate in case things turned unexpectedly. The next day, a staggering and disappointing blow followed. The whole of the Russian force was in full retreat to Russia, leaving the Assyrians they had just rescued at the mercy of their enemies. The Russian general and his officers were completely taken by surprise, for the order had come from the highest command. The order was dictated by the very threatening state of events in Trans-Caucasia, where Envar Pasha, at the head of the main Turkish Army, was threatening Batum. The Turkish invasion was utterly defeated at Sara Kamish, but this fact was of no benefit to the Christians in Urmia. The Russians had gone and did not intend to return for the time being.

Panic ruled in Urmia and the neighboring districts. In Tergawar district, along the borderline of Turkey and Persia, the village of Mar Bhishu was on either side of the border. The Assyrians of the Turkish side and Persian side would cross back and forth. This was especially true for young and playful boys and girls. Sergei Kaku, whose name in Assyrian was Arsanis, was nine years of age in 1914–1915. He was from Mar Bhishu on the Turkish side. But to the native inhabitants of these regions, Turkey or Persia meant nothing. They were Assyrian mountaineers. This was their ancestral land. From Lake Van to Lake Urmia, from the River Tigris to the River Zab, they called themselves "Atooray." They were the people of "Atoor," those who lived in "Toora," meaning "mountains," the name that ancient Greeks called "Assur," the once powerful empire between the tenth to seventh centuries B.C. This empire was most often mentioned in the Bible as a warrior nation. But the people were also the builders of Babylon and translators of the Sumerian culture.

The dark clouds from the panic in Urmia were not far from Mar Bhishu. Many Christians who were able to do so followed in the track of the retreating Russian troops. About 10,000 fled to Russia, finding safety in this way. Those who could not were crowded in various mission yards, particularly into the missions that were run by Americans. The attitude of local Mussalmans soon became very threatening. Sixty Assyrian men were marched from the town of Urmia to the village of Gulpasha and all but two were put to death. Initially, all 60 of them were offered life on the condition that they accept Islam. Two of the men accepted and a few days later they reverted. Afterwards, they faced death for having become Muslims and reverted to Christianity, for no Muslim can revert to any other religion. There were other slaughters on the "hill of the Jews" in the village of Charbash. And during such times, Sergei Kaku (Arsanis) lost all of his family members and was orphaned at age 9.

On the Persian side of Mar Bhishu, a pregnant young woman named "Betashva" or "Betsy", was hiding inside a cave just outside of "Kala Ismail Agha," several miles from Urmia. Jackals and wolves were always close by. She was thirsty, hungry, and cold. She was also nine months pregnant. Being an Assyrian villager, she worked until the last moment of pregnancy. Resting before child birth was a privilege that was non-existent in such villages. During child birth, a nanny and at some point, a few other women from the village would assist a mother in labor. Betsy was alone for three days inside a dark and damp cave. How long her labor lasted is not known. What is known is that she gave birth to a set of twin daughters with no names. How many more days her family was alive together is not known. Who was the first to die, the mother or the infant child, is also not known. At some point during the many days of massacre, a small group of armed Assyrian men and woman made their pass by the cave. A few Assyrian cavalry men heard the echo of a crying child. By the time they reached the family of three, however, the child had passed out. They knew Betsy and Mikhael. They found Betsy and her two infants dead by the mouth of the cave. Betsy had dragged herself and the infants to the mouth of the cave. In the Assyrian tradition of burial, the Assyrian men washed the mother and two infants. However, one of the infants shivered and began to scream. The group gave the infant the name of "Shimuni," the female version of "Shimun," or Simon.

• • •

Turkey

That day, the site in the hills of "Kala Ismail Agha," where Sonia was born, was horrid. Seventy Assyrian men from Gawar were brought there, tied up in bunches, and handed over to a gang of Kurds to be knifed and clubbed to death. Their bodies were left to the jackals until a group of American missionaries were able to get to them and give their bones at least a decent burial. The winter of 1914 to 1915 was a dark one in Urmia.

The people of Gawar were "Toorayeh," or mountaineers, like the people of "Tkhumeh," or the people of "Tyareh," and the people of "Diz." In the fourth century A.D., the emperor Constantine sent a few contingents of these mountaineers to the present-day Catalonia. In the annals of Catalonians, these warriors were named as "Alma Gawar," which in the Assyrian language means "people of Gawar." In the mountains of Hakkary and its surroundings, the Turks were avoiding trouble with the Assyrian mountaineers for the moment. After the Turkish defeat at Sara Kamish, the Turks had removed any idea of invading Russian territory from their minds. Besides, the Russian advance on Van and Erzrum, which means "the land of Rome," was becoming more and more probable. If such an advance took place, the flanking position of the Assyrian mountaineers was a fearful thing to think about.

By now, the Armenian massacres were in full swing. The Turks were resolved to continue these massacres; however, the presence of American missionaries made it impossible for the Turks to openly deny the massacres. From the annals of Talaat, it is written that first the Minister of the Interior, and later Grand Vizir, had declared to "settle this Armenian question for the next 50 years at least." Even though there was no fighting in the mountains between the Turks and the Assyrians at the time, but a good deal of dread toward the future was still on the horizon. As a precaution, the patriarchal family, and later the Patriarch himself, left the isolated village of Qudshanis and moved to the Ashiret district of Diz and to the relative safety of its rugged mountains.

In the Name of Life

In the spring of 1915 the Russian troops advanced and took what remained of the city of Van, which was in ruins after the desperate fighting between the Armenian Dashnakists and the Turkish government troops. The city was the scene of the most awful massacres by the Turks. The great American mission building was completely destroyed. In April, the Russians sent deputation to Bashkala and Julamerk, calling on the Assyrian mountaineers to rise and fight for the Christians against the Mussalmans, who had proclaimed the general jihad. Shortly after, the Russians re-occupied Urmia. A meeting of notable Assyrians was held in Diz, and the men of the mountains had to make a definitive choice. Fearing that the Sunni Turks and Sunni Kurds would join, and that the Turks might not be able to defend them from the Kurds, it was ultimately decided, upon receiving Russian promises, that they would throw in their lot with the Entente against Turkey.

The Assyrian mountaineer confederation of districts was called to arms on the 10th of May, 1915. A definite and formal declaration of war was sent by the leaders of the newly established mountaineer nation to the Vali of Var. As soon as the Assyrians committed themselves, the Russians withdrew to Van and left their mountain allies to fend for themselves. The peril became real at once. Qudshanis was attacked and burned by the Kurds. The patriarchal library and the English mission both shared the common lot. The books and other documents, which had been concealed in what was held to be a safe place, were found and destroyed. The Turkish authorities had not lost hope of having discussions with the Assyrian mountaineers. The Kaimmakam of Julamerk, Rajib Raghab Bey, whose name means "with great authority," sent frequent messages to the Patriarch at Diz. All was fruitless. A Deacon, Shamasha Ephraim, even wrote a war song which was chanted from village to village among the hills. In the meantime, two orphan Assyrians, a boy, Arsanis (Sergei) 9 years old, and an infant, Shimuni (Sonia), only few months old, were destined to have a life where the grown-ups slew each other.

The Assyrians of the mountain districts could only get a few rifles and cartridges from their Russian allies. The mountaineers stood holding at bay, among their crags and gorges, largely superior forces of Kurds and regular Turkish troops from Mosul. By the middle of May and before the end of June, the Assyrians were to be attacked from many directions. The Berwar Kurds, backed by a garrison of Turkish troops from Mosul, attacked on the Lizan valley of lower Tiari, while Artosh Kurds, led by Kaimmakam of Julamerk, attacked Chumba. On the other side of the Zab, the Agha of Chal had brought his forces against Salabekan and Tkhumeh. Sutu of Oramar, old enemy of the Assyrians, and was taking the field against Jilu and Baz. Somehow the fighting spirit of these Assyrian mountaineers was not broken; their moral was high, and they did not lose all of the territories.

On the whole, this formidable series of attacks failed or were only partially successful. The Lizan valley was occupied with the village of Ashitha, but the attacks on Chumba d'Malik, Jilua, and Salabekan were repulsed with heavy loss to the Kurds. Five days later, the onset was renewed and a severe fighting at Sawa, on the Zab, was in progress. The bridge was retaken by the Assyrians, then finally taken and held again by the Kurds. The Kurds were never able to improve their position and cross the Zab.

The result of a week of severe fighting was that the Assyrians had lost the districts on the right, or western bank of the Zab, but were able to destroy the bridges and maintain their position on the other bank. The Patriarch Mar Shimun, during the few days pause, visited Diza and Gawar, and got in touch with the Russians in Van and Urmia. The Patriarch was able to bring a small number of rifles and ammunition, but not much more. The brother of Mar Shimun, Hormizd, was in Constantinople (Istanbul) for studies and was arrested and sent to Mosul when Turkey entered the struggle. Haidar Beg Vali of Mosul sent a message to Mar Shimun—"your brother is in my hand, and unless the Assyrians lay down their arms, your brother will die." The reply was this: "How could we give up so many for one?" Hormizd was put to death.

In the Name of Life

The Russians sent a detachment of 400 Cossacks from Urmia to help the Assyrian mountaineers. The commander was ignorant of the territory and allowed himself to be the guest of Sutu, the Agha of Oramar, arch-enemy of the Assyrians. Sutu sent a message to Shiekh Seyyid Mahommed to cut off the Russians at the "Galia Balanda," or "deep gorge." During this treacherous fighting, the Russians were massacred, and one of the sons of Sutu was killed and Sutu himself was wounded. Once more, the Assyrian mountaineers were left on their own to face a second attack. This was delivered in August, 1915 with the help of the Barzan Kurds. The Barzanies forgot how the Christian Assyrian Ashirets helped their former chief, Shiekh Selim, when he was a fugitive from the Turks, and eventually the Ottoman government executed him. The Kurdish attack succeeded and the villages of Tkhomeh, Tiari, Jilu, and Baz were ravaged pitilessly. All the courtesies of tribal war were neglected. In Jihad war, which is in the name of Allah, some Muslims believe that they can commit any atrocities that they might think of. That is not what Islam was. It was only now, that the famous church of Mar Zeia in Jilu was plundered—for the first time in its history—even 700 years after Islam began. It is believed that a written linen of protection, which carried an autographed letter of the Prophet himself, was a sufficient shield for the shrine even in the days of Bedr Khan Beg and his ravages. Now, however, even that had failed. A certain fanatical young Kurdish Agha of the Shekak Kurds, the eldest son of the chief, Simco, as he stood at the church door superintending the removal of the plunder, was shot in the head and killed.

Besides the atrocities toward the Christian population, some 40 churches in Jilu alone were plundered. The sacred prize, the seventh-century jars brought from China by Assyrian Christian missions in that country would have been worth their weight in gold to the Turk's allies, the Germans. Though beaten from their valleys, the Assyrians had not lost hope for life and were still unbroken in spirit. Attacked again and again, the Kurds were repeatedly beaten back. Sallying parties of Assyrians were even able to venture down into the villages and bring back some small stores of corn. These Christians had food for a while, the flocks were with them still, and water was abundant in that land where the snowdrifts never melt.

It was late December of the year 1915, at the altitude of 10,000 feet where the Assyrian mountaineers encamped. Life had become impossible on the heights. Mar Shimun and a small group of mountaineers accomplished a daring journey and arrived in the district of Salmas. Unfortunately, in the district of Gawar, the Kurdish chief Nuri Beg had just carried out a cruel massacre against unarmed Christians. In Salmas, the local Russian officers had urged Mar Shimun not to go back to the heights. But to no avail, he went back to share the fate of his 25,000 men, women and children mountaineers. The territory remains one of the most rugged places in the world. The bulk of Kurds were to the east of these mountaineers, guarding the direct road to Persia, and drawing their food from the fertile plain of Gawar.

It was determined by Mar Shimun to go in the opposite direction of the Kurds, marching down the valleys of Diz and Tal, to cross Zab by the two bridges near the foot of those gorges. The two columns could then unite in the district of Berwar, north of Qudshanis, a day's march from the district of Albaq. Against all odds, they crossed Zab and broke the bridges behind them. The Kurds had made their way across a natural bridge, Hezekian, and were chasing the Assyrians. But there was a last sharp action in the hills and Khoshaba (Sunday) of Lizan distinguished himself and defeated the Kurds. This opened the way to the comparative safety of the district of Albaq, and from there the Assyrians could gradually make their way to the Persian district of Salmas. The Mountaineers had deliberately, and in the face of great temptation and danger, thrown in their lot with what they believed to be their right, in the name of life. They stood and defended themselves against tremendous odds to save a few remnants of an ancient culture. They stood and defended a few mothers, daughters, and orphans. They stood and fought to spare a few generations before the last of the Assyrians vanished.

Arsanis (Sergei), which is an extraction of the name Sargon (one of the ancient Assyrian and Babylonian kings), survived by following the flocks and picking up any scraps that the starving population could afford to give him. He had the love of his people and knew they would do everything that is humanly possible to keep him as one of their own children. He had lost his father, mother, and two sisters, and was all alone. He was only nine. By this time, he had seen and experienced enough cruelty to last him a lifetime. To ascend and descend the hills of a rugged territory without shoes or warm clothing would have been enough, but to face the constant fear of being massacred was most inhumane.

Arsanis was separated from his mother and his two elder sisters during the escape of 1915. He would never see them again. He was a child in the midst of an international political storm, with the Turks and the Germans on the one hand and the Russians, French, and English on the other, dividing the world of hate and cruelty. Arsanis was born in a world where a child's innocence was held in the balance of various Imperial, political corruptions.

Infant Shimuni (Sonia) was adopted by escaping mothers, nursed by a few of them, and was brought back to life. Mothers would lose their infants during their marches due to the lack of nutrition and cold. An infant to share was a gift from God. The cry of a child, in moments of desperation, could be the loving sign of life. In the desert, a blade of grass is a jewel. A child is not a Muslim, a Christian, or a Jew. It is a scale in the name of life, a measurement so rare that is blessed by no less than all that is nature. All are blessed to be born as a child, but some may choose to die something much worse.

Though beaten from their home land, these mountaineers were no more crushed than the Serbs were in a similar case. The mountaineers conducted an orderly retreat in the face of what they had encountered and were still able to bring down their families as well as their second most important asset, their flocks and herds. The Assyrian mountaineers arrived in Persia, not knowing what would be the next turn of fortune's wheel.

Persia

In theory, Persia was a sovereign and independent nation. However, it was ruled by a government too feeble to act neutrally with respect to the Assyrian mountaineers. Besides, Persia was a Shiite country and followed Islamic rules. Urmia had been, in fact, the headquarters of a small Russian garrison and arsenals. The first act of the war was the Turkish (Sunni) invasion of the district that had been repelled by the Russians and by some subjects of Persian (Shiite) extraction, but emphatically not by the Persian Government, Qajar, of Turkish extraction. Urmia, in theory, was still an important provincial town of Persia, ruled by a governor nominated by the Prince of Azerbaijan, who had always been the heir-apparent of Persia. But Urmia was also the residence of a Russian consul, and a very considerable garrison which was under his command. The Consul took his official counsel from the Assyrian council (Mutwa). This was a reversal of the days when Assyrians were in a state of subjection. The climate was toxic even before, but now, with arrival of 25,000 mountaineers who had lost everything, a storm of religious persecution was on the horizon.

As reported by the American mission, the mountaineers behaved much better than might have reasonably been expected. In the district of Salmas, under the eye of the Patriarch, the Shiite population even complimented these refugees, basically a homeless population, for their behavior, discipline, and pride. The situation, nonetheless, was very tense. A hungry population of 25,000, when thrown upon any establishment by a chance war they had nothing to do with, will help themselves regardless of race, color, or religion if help does not arrive.

The Governor, who was a member of the Royal House of Persia, was proceeding from Tabriz to Urmia to take up his post, to which he had been newly appointed, with an escort of three hundred cavalry. Passing the northern end of Lake Urmia where the road turned abruptly around the nose of a rock, he found a party of 200 mountaineers peacefully sitting by the roadside, who saluted him as he drove past. Without the least provocation, coming simply from the general state of panic that made him see a murderer in every mountaineer, he ordered his escort loose upon them, allowing his soldiers to massacre, pillage, and commit outrages as they liked while he sat in the carriage and looked on.

From that moment on, the mountaineers did not sit idle. Their families were in a dire situation. They conducted a series of well-arranged raids against the Kurds. They sacked the stronghold of Sutu Agha, at Oramar, during a well-planned raid. They attacked Chal under the leadership of David, brother of the Patriarch, and took many Kurds, including the son of Agha, as their prisoners. There was a broad, informal truce in the Urmia district from the January of 1916 until the end of the following year. The Russians, recognizing the art of survivability of the Assyrians, sent a fair supply of rifles, ammunition, and of course decorations, which were prized and worn by the mountaineers. Personal congratulations of the Tsar were sent to Mar-Shimun, who visited Tiflis to receive high decorations from the Grand Duke Nicholas himself.

The Assyrians were holding their own, with or without the permission of Persia, Turkey, or the Kurds. They did not understand the international laws. Such orders had never protected them. They were not sophisticated people. They believed, followed, and mostly died, not so much for just being Christians but also because of the brutal international politics played out thousands of miles away. Their Patriarch was a reflection of the past and not a shrewd politician of the changing world, with new and modern killing machines. They were lucky if they had a rifle and few bullets. They had nothing else to stand on but faith. Oftentimes, however, faith is a weak substitute for guns and bullets. Even though since the times of antiquity these were their ancestral lands, now the Assyrian barely existed as a corporate body of the land and were at the mercy of their Muslim neighbors, who were at war among themselves. The Assyrians continued their scattered existence in Persia until the autumn of 1917, when the unmistakable signs of the complete collapse of Tsarist Russia and the Romanov dynasty began to show and aroused well-founded anxiety.

The Russian allies of that time, the French and British, made sure to occupy the power vacuum in the Caucasus. A Franco-British military mission had been dispatched to the Trans-Caucasus region in preparation for a great military blow to the Turks from that direction. The position of the Assyrians in Urmia was known to the Franco-British mission. The plan was to create a line of defense, extending from the Black Sea to the Persian Gulf, to block the known German designs on India. General Offley Shore's idea was to use the Armenians of Van, the Assyrians of Urmia, and Chief Simco, Agha of the Shekak Kurds, whose territory consisted of the range of mountains that separated the two Lakes of Van and Urmia. Simco, whose actual Kurdish name was Ismail, was leader to 2,000 mounted men. He had held the rank of colonel of Hamidie in the Turkish service. His elder brother, Jaffar Agha, was murdered by the heir-apparent (Vali-ahd) of Azerbaijan, the same Governor that ordered the massacre of 200 innocent Assyrian mountaineers during his procession from Tabiz to Urmia. Simco had declared that he would never trust a Persian again. Simco would insist that the British consuls come and dine with him, whether they would accept his hospitality or not. He claimed that when a Kurd invites you, it would be impolite not to accept the invitation. Once, he carried his friendship so far as to offer Captain Dickson, R.A., the British Consul at Van, his latest married wife against a Mannlicher rifle owned by the Consul.

General Shore believed he could win Simco's allegiance. The Armenian commander in Van, Hambartsunian, had his deepest suspicions about Simco. But General Shore and two British Intelligence Officers, Captain Gracey, and Lieut. McDowell overruled Hambartsunian. The two Intelligence officers were dispatched to Simco's stronghold at Chara. Simco swore on the Koran to fight for the English, Kurds, and Armenians in fellowship with Mar-Shimun, whom he declared that he regarded as the honorary head of Kurdistan. Mar-Shimun admitted to Captain Gracey that he shared Hambartsunian's doubts about Simco's honesty. However, the agreement was made with Simco and Captain Gracey was sent to Urmia to make arrangements with the Assyrians. The meeting was held on the American mission's premises and Dr. Shedd presided over it. The scheme was that 250 Russian officers were to be sent to organize the Assyrian forces to form part of Black Sea Baghdad line. The assent of Persian Government had been secured with some growling, but at the end the Assyrians yielded gladly to "force majeure." Of course, money and munitions were to be sent both to the Persians and the newly-formed alliance, the Black Sea–Persian Gulf defense line against the Germans.

A mountaineers' army was hastily formed and made to advance from Urmia to Khoi to meet the expected Persian succor force, which never arrived. The Assyrian expedition force then returned to Urmia. It wasn't hard to figure out that even though the defense plan was interesting, it had no touch with reality. The historically unprecedented fact that the whole Russian Empire was collapsing gradually became undeniable. This wasn't the case of a strong wall just falling, but rather one where the bricks that made the wall were disintegrating back to the original mud from which they were made.

Unfortunately for the Assyrians, Russia had collapsed and the British were far away in the south, out of reach. The Persian authorities now took an air of high virtue and ordered the Assyrians to lay down their arms. Russia was gone and the British could not help. If the Assyrians were to lay down their arms, a massacre was certain.

The Assyrians naturally declined. Persia was in no position to guarantee protection to anyone. Mar-Shimun sent an explanatory letter to Vali-Ahd (heir-apparent) of Persia and to an English educated gentleman, Mukht-i-shems, Governor of Tabriz. The Vali-Ahd was the same man who ordered the massacre of 200 innocent Assyrian mountaineers in Urmia during his procession from Tabriz to Urmia. Mar-Shimun explained that the Assyrians were merely refugees in Persian territory, who carried arms solely to protect their loved ones and themselves. The situation was most unstable and the combustion of centuries of disagreements reached its "flash-point" and the inevitable religious explosion occurred on February 16, 1918.

Two days of sharp fighting took place in the streets of Urmia, between what were once neighbors and friends, claiming many lives from both sides. The Muslims were utterly put down and Urmia, at least for the time being, remained under the Council of Christians (Mutwa) of which the Patriarch Mar-Shimun was the official head. The Patriarch had distinguished himself by both his efforts to keep peace before the outbreak and by saving lives during it. The Persian Government had had a lesson to the effect that the Assyrians, even though cut off from Russia, were yet a formidable adversary for the Persian Government to deal with. The Persian Government took to assassination.

Mukht-i-shems, a thoroughly westernized Persian gentleman, had been in communication with Simco Agha through a signed letter, which told him plainly that if he could remove Mar-Shimun, the Persian Government would esteem it as a good service for the country. Simco, profiting from the hint, sent a letter to Mar-Shimun, who resided in Salmas, suggesting that the two needed to meet in a certain village, conducted safely by his mounted men, to discuss in secret some matter of urgency. They were sworn allies who should discuss the new situation caused by the Russian debacle. The Patriarch agreed to meet Simco at the village of Koni Shehr. On February 25, 1918, Mar-Shimun, his brother David, and a few friends went to meet their sworn allies. Simco was hospitable and cordial. He showed the utmost respect to "the religious head of Kurdistan." After discussions, Simco escorted his guest to his carriage, kissed his hand out of courtesy, and turned back into the house. That was the sign. Next came one shot, and then a volley from Simco's men who were posted on the roof. The Patriarch lay dead in his carriage, a victim to his trust in the honor of a Kurd who claimed to have hated the Persians. David survived and was sheltered in the house of an Armenian woman until he was able to escape next morning. The Patriarch's body was treated with gross indignity, stripped and flung out into the street before finally being taken up by the Armenians of the village and given a Christian burial by an Armenian priest in their own church.

The Assyrians did not remain quiescent under such provocation. A force was dispatched to avenge their Patriarch, led by his brother David, Khoshaba of Tiari, and Petros of Baz. Petros was a born leader of irregular Assyrian troops, so much so that the Kurds gave him the title of "Agha" Petros. Under Petros, Simco was utterly defeated and his castle at Chara, in the district of Salmas, was captured. Simco escaped and remained in hiding for a long time. In Simco's castle there were private papers including a letter from the Governor of Tabriz suggesting the murder of the Patriarch.

The Government of Persia was ruled by the non-Persian Qajar dynasty. This royal dynasty was of Turkish origin, specifically from the Qajar tribe. The Qajar dynasty permanently lost much of Persia's integral territory to Russia over the course of the 19th century, comprising modern-day Georgia, Dagestan, Azerbaijan, and Armenia; Georgia and Armenia being Christian, and Dagestan and Azerbaijan being Muslim. The Qajar Turkic family ruled over a Shiite Persia, while Turkey and Kurds are Sunni. It is as if there is a curse in these lands. Not only do the Shiite and Sunni fight, but the Christians also have strife among themselves. The Armenians of the Caucasus were at open war with those of Turkey, and the former, who were hoping for peace with the Central Powers, were tainted with Bolshevism. To make matters worse, there was another line of division. This was the renewal of an old quarrel between the two Armenian revolutionary societies, the "Dashnak" and the "Huntchak." One of the most skillful leaders of the Armenians in the Van district was Andranik. He found himself abandoned by the Russians when he attempted to face the Turks with Armenian troops. The Russian Armenians abandoned him in the face of his enemy, the Turks. It got so bad that the Dashnaks sought to murder him on the field of battle. Under such a line of

Persia

fissure, the Turkish army advanced on Erzerum and recaptured an extremely important place without any opposition, and helped themselves to all the guns, rifles, ammunition, and transport which Entente had forwarded to Russia for the Russian advance.

Andranik had a following of 5,000 men. He struck south, hoping to join with the Assyrians in Urmia where Agha Petros was now in full command. The plan could have worked. Both Andranik and Petros showed the capacity of good guerilla leaders, but not good politicians. The Assyrians were mountaineers and wild. The Armenians were more disciplined. The Turks, who held the interior line, were preventing Andranik's march to join the Assyrians. The two Christian troops had planned to meet between Salmas and Khoi. Petros and the Turkish leader, and Ali Ihsan Bey were about to clash, but the Turks turned back and headed to meet the Armenians in Khoi. There was desperate street fighting at Khoi. Andranik was unable to restraint his own fighting ardor and plunged into the center of the town, leaving his troops leaderless just when a general was needed to outflank the movement of his enemies. Andranik withdrew to Julfa and the Caucasus, where he remained till the end of the war.

The courage of the Assyrians was far from being broken, even though the Turks were able to prevent the junction of their troops and the Armenians in the district of Van. For three months, they kept the field against a confederacy of Turks, Persians, and Kurds under the leadership of Petros, beating off a series of attacks, both to the north and south of Urmia. In one of these battles near the Ushnu, they captured 325 prisoners of Turkish regular army, and a large number of Kurdish tribesmen. Twenty-four of these prisoners were Turkish officers. The Assyrians also took five machine guns and two field guns as the spoils of war. The Assyrians, to their credit, treated all of their regular prisoners well and released them within a few days. Even more remarkable, these mountaineers, who had no military discipline, knew that if the case was reversed, the Turkish officers would not have been so humane toward the Assyrians. The Turkish commander in Salmas,

Jevdet Bey, who was previously Vali of Van, had forced the inhabitants of an Assyrian village to dig a deep ditch at the foot of a mud wall. He marched 700 men, women, and children into the ditch that they had dug with their own hands, and buried the whole population of the village alive. The Assyrians spared the Turkish prisoners, having those recollections fresh in their mind, proclaiming that they will not shame their Christian name in like retaliation.

This wasn't the case with the respect to the Kurds. After the disrespectful murder and treatment of Mar-Shimun's corpse, there was national condemnation of the Kurds. Assyrians took no Kurdish prisoners. They remembered what had been done after the Assyrians had fired their last cartridge, and when the Kurds had surrounded a small village only two days' journey from Urmia. The Kurds had sworn on the Koran that if the villagers lay down their arms, their lives would be spared. Every man was massacred, and every female between the ages of 6 and 60 was ravished and turned out naked as they made their way to Urmia. This is where Arsanis' mother and two elder sisters died. They never made it to Urmia. His father and two uncles were killed in the wars of the Mountaineers.

The fighting continued. The isolated Assyrians could hope for no more than to repulse the confederation of their enemies. Their military stores were limited. The ammunition soon began to run perilously low. Their end, which was nothing less than absolute destruction, was in sight and the holding position was hopeless. On July 18, 1918, a true "deus ex machina" appeared to save the situation. This was a British airplane piloted by Capt. Pennington. He had started in Miani, 150 miles south of Urmia. He was flying over unknown territory and hostile country, trying to find a place to land. He flew over Urmia. The Assyrians, believing that this airplane was Turkish, started firing and Capt. Pennington came under heavy fire from all manner of weapons. The pilot escaped the bullets and finally landed, only to run a further risk of suffocation from the Assyrian crowd that pressed upon him to kiss him.

The pilot was wearing shorts, which to the Assyrian woman from Urmia only meant that this poor soul must have met with some disaster and they insisted on making a pair of trousers for him.

A few British Cavalry had been pushed up from their base around Bagdad to see if anything could be done to help the Assyrians and Capt. Pennington was no more than a far advance scout. He had brought, at least, a coherent plan of action with him. If the Assyrians could hold onto Urmia a bit longer, officers, munitions, and money would be sent to enable them to sustain themselves. A first installment of these promises was made at Sain Kaleh, about 150 kilometers to the south. The problem was that Urmia was threatened by a force of two Turkish divisions, the 5th and the 6th, stationed respectively to the north and south of the town. In addition, there were a large number of Persian and Kurdish irregulars. The British force at Sain Kaleh had orders not to go beyond that point, but the officers had still hoped to help the Assyrians in Urmia. The British force consisted of no more than a squadron of cavalry, the 14th Hussars, and a machine gun company. They could hardly be expected to push their way alone toward Urmia. The only thing left for the Assyrians of Urmia to do was to march to the south and break their way through the 6th Turkish division of the Ottomans at Saj Bulak and contain them. Then, a detachment of the Assyrians, to be sent to Sain Kaleh, was to bring in the promised supplies. This is what was discussed between Captain Bennington and Petros and his men. Captain Bennington departed on the 19th of July and the Assyrian detachment was to meet the English at Sain Kaleh on the 23rd of July.

Petros marched out with the Urmia division of his army, leaving the Salmas division to guard his northern front. Even though Petros had never studied at a military school, he had talent, skill, and daring. He completely defeated the Turkish Ottoman 6th division at Saj Bulak and forced it to retreat to the hills of Rowanduz. If he only had left the bulk of his force to "contain" the defeated Ottoman enemy and passed the message to Urmia of the Assyrian victory, all could have been won. But Petros could not resist the temptation of a short, yet triumphant march to greet the British at Sain kaleh. If Petros had studied at a military school, he would have known not to leave an enemy in the rear, defeated but not annihilated.

The Ottoman 5th division, to the north of Urmia, realizing that Salmas division was the only thing guarding the city, attacked immediately. Disorganized, unaware of their victory over the 6th Ottoman division and leaderless, they lost the line of the Nazlu River and fell back to the city. A general panic ensued and all the Christian population of Urmia evacuated the city, not unlike the Roman followers of Pompeii during Julius Caesar's march on Rome. The Assyrians poured down the southern road to Sain Kaleh. Somewhere between 50,000 to 70,000 men, women, and children took to the southern road. In this march, it wasn't the case of each man for himself but rather each tribe for itself. After over 2,500 years of not having a national entity, the Assyrians had very little sense of national unity and duty. It was more that they recognized a sense of obligation to their own village or tribe. Again, this is not unlike many Germanic tribes, or the highlanders in England of a few hundred years ago. They would join for an attack on a common enemy, but still, to a Cameron, Stewart, or MacDonald, a national discipline, for the sake of a national duty was not a priority.

Naturally, their opponents were on their track at once. The Kurds and the Persians came down on the scattered Assyrians like wolves upon a herd of sheep. There was 150 kilometers of plunder and massacre in which no mercy was shown. Men were slaughtered; women were stripped and violated, then killed. Girls were carried off to Muslim harems. Twenty-five percent of the Assyrians perished in only few days.

The mountaineers did better than the plainsmen. The mountaineers of Tiari brought their families, and even their sheep, back to their mountains. They held their military cohesion and discipline. They brought more sheep back than they had in the beginning, having collected them from the Kurdish villages that they defeated on their return to the mountains. Petros arrived on the 30th of July in Sain Kaleh. In some cultures, time is not that important. Obviously, that was the case for Petros. He was seven days late. He was initially quite undisturbed, until he discovered that the small British force, waiting a few days at the most extreme risk, had commenced to retreat to the south and that nobody was at the rendezvous site. However, the British were only one day to the south and were prepared to deliver the supplies as had been arranged. Upon hearing news of the Urmia evacuation, the British Commander ordered a return to Sain Kaleh, finding thousands of Assyrians being massacred on the road under the leadership of a Qajar Royal family member of Persia, Mejid-es-Sultaneh, Ottoman 5th division and Kurdish and Persian irregulars. The British troops arrived on the 3rd of August.

More than 50,000 refugees arrived in Sain Kaleh under the British protection and charity. The Kurds and Persians were on their tracks, thirsty for blood, certain that they could get revenge and plunder to their heart's content. The Kurds were taken by surprise upon their arrival to Sain Kaleh, by a squadron of cavalry and a machine gun company that was awaiting them. This was a different story than facing a horde of unarmed men and women. There were three days of fighting, as the cavalry covered the passage of the refugees who were still arriving in streams. A strong force of Kurds was harrying a number of refugees when a party of only seven soldiers, three officers and four B.O.R.'s, appeared upon the scene. These seven men, without hesitation, dashed into the midst of the Kurds with a Lewis gun upon their saddles, dismounted, and opened fire into the fleeing Kurds. The British leader, Captain Savage, secured a well-earned D.S.O. for the feat of courage, and Captain Scott Ollson was awarded the Military Cross.

The Kurds and the Ottoman Turks withdrew, abandoning their Assyrian prey. Dr. Shedd, the American missionary at Sain Kaleh, died of typhus, helping the Assyrian refugees until the end. If the

Assyrians stayed in the region, they would perish. The decision was made to march the Assyrians of Urmia to Hamadan and Kirmanshah, where they would be within reach of British protection.

Hamadan was a new name for the ancient city of "Ekbatan," in Persia. The city of Ekbatan was the Eastern Capital of the Assyrian Empire during the 7th century B.C. In the language of "Assyrian" (also in the ancient Persian language of "Pahlavi"), Ekbatan comes from "Akh-Betan," meaning "like our house." Like most forced marches, the march was dangerous and uninviting, especially as such multitudes of refugees had no food supplies. It is frankly admitted that the Assyrians plundered whatever they could find of supplies and food. They were a starving crowd, but still armed men who had lost all that they ever had and there was still the proclamation of "Jihad" against them. However, more to the Assyrian credit, though the memories of their wives and daughters were fresh in their minds when they were fallen in the hands of their enemy, in no single instance was there even complaint that a Muslim woman had met with insult or mistreatment at the hands of the Christians.

The Assyrians reached Hamadan, where the irregular levies they had formed were taken under the control of British officers, including a few Assyrian "Amazon ladies." These ladies would ride astride their horses with rifles at their backs and revolvers at their hips. They made the most efficient officers. Even the wildest of men somehow respect a motherly or sisterly figure. The Assyrians were eventually brought from Hamadan to Baquba, about 30 miles from Bagdad. The British officers had nothing but praises for the endurance and cheerfulness of the mountaineer battalion. The Assyrian battalion brigaded with the picked Indian troops "Garwhalis."

Between the years 1914 to 1921, Persia was on the verge of disintegration, having been ravaged by the corrupt government of Ahmad Shah of the Qajar dynasty. Russia and England had strong commercial and political interests in the country. Qajar, being a

Turkish dynasty, was often opposed by political movements of Persian descent. The end of Qajar finally came at the hands of one of the Persian military men when Reza-Khan, as he was initially known from the Mazanderan province of the Caspian Sea, revolted against Ahmad Shah. On February 21, 1921, at the head of 1,200 men, Reza-Khan occupied Tehran, while Ahmad Shah was undergoing a lengthy cure in Europe, mostly in England. Reza-Khan brought his men and a few cannons by the gates of Majlis (Ahmad Shah's Parliament), and demanded the deposition of the ill-fated king, who was nowhere to be found. A young journalist, Sayyid-zia al-Din Tabataba'I, became prime minister, and Reza-Khan became the commander of all forces and the Minister of War. In the year 1923, Reza-Khan became the prime minister. Two years later, in 1925, Majlis deposed Ahmad Shah and in April, 1926, Reza-Khan was elected to become the Shah of Iran, as Reza-Shah Pahlavi.

In 1921, Sergei was 16-years-old and had found the only living member of his family, his Uncle Ivan, in Kiev. By now, Sergei had been living with his uncle for three years. Sergei had marched for three treacherous years across the Trans-Caucasian, Russian, and Ukrainian territories. From 1915 until the end of 1918, he endured a life that no child should. He was able to keep up with most of the Assyrian refugees moving through the Eastern Turkey, Azerbaijan, Tiflis, Rostov, Donetsk, and Kharkov, and finally made it to Kiev with a group of a few hundred Assyrians.

The Assyrian network precedes today's global communications network. The Assyrians communicated across many countries and knew who was related to whom, at times even knowing more personal information than was desired. Ivan Kaku was a member of the cavalry mountaineers of Mar-Shimun. He was born in Russia and raised in Ukraine but joined the mountaineer's cavalry of Mar-Shimun to fight in Turkey and Persia. He was informed that only a single child survived from his brother's family. Ivan searched many of the Assyrian refugee camps in the hope of finding Sergei. Typhoid was prevalent in most of the camps. Having given up any hope of finding the child, he married and settled in Kiev. One day, at the end of 1918, a few Assyrians knocked on his door and presented him with 13-year-old Sergei.

In 1916, Mikhael Nona reached Kharkov with his two sons and a 4-year-old daughter whose back was badly injured by galloping Kurdish hoards during the massacre of "Kala Ismail Agha." The family escaped into the hills and joined other Assyrian villagers who were in the same predicament. The family was split. "Betsy," the mother of the children, had died after giving birth to twins, one of whom survived and adopted by a group of Assyrians. The killing began in the late afternoon and continued until late into the night.

Six months later, a group of Assyrians who were able to cross the Trans-Caucasia with the Russian troops in 1916 knocked on Mikhael Nona's door and delivered Shimuni to her father and the remaining family. In the year 1921, Shimuni was six years of age and growing up in Kharkov. By now, her name was Sonia.

A year later, in 1922, the Ottoman Empire had seen the departure of its last Sultan, Mehmed VI. In October, 1923, Ali Riza Oglu Mustafa, known worldwide as Mustafa Kemal Ataturk (the father of Turkey), became Turkey's first president. Ataturk organized the Turkish nationalistic movement that created the new secular Republic of Turkey. Unlike its predecessor, the Ottoman Empire, the government was no longer led by a hereditary monarchy or religious leaders. Not only was Sultan Mehmed VI removed, but the Caliphate was also abolished. The last Caliph of Turkey was Abdulmecid II. In 1924. Turkey signed the Treaty of Lausanne, recognizing minority religions.

PRELUDE TO WORLD WAR II

Russia

The Romanov dynasty had ended, and in the year 1922 the Soviet Union was created by uniting Russia, Ukraine, Belarus, and the Trans-Caucasian former Persian territories of Armenia, Georgia, and Azerbaijan. Two years of famine killed five million of the Soviet population. In 1924, the Soviet Union adopted a constitution based on dictatorship. Lenin died in 1924 and was succeeded by Stalin (Stalin, in the Russian language, translates into *forged through steal*). In 1929 Stalin called for collectivization and ordered the persecution of "Kulaks" or rich farmers, as well as the deportation of 15 million farmers to the Arctic regions, where 6.5 million died. In December of that same year, 1.8 million were convicted of other crimes.

In the year 1930, Sergei Kaku of Kiev, 25 years old, married Sonia Nona of Kharkov, 15 years old. In the tradition of the Assyrians, Sergei gave Mikhael, Sonia's father, 150 Tsar Nicholas gold pieces on a silver platter. That was an incredible sum of wealth, considering that Sergei was only 25 years old and an orphan. Now "Shimuni," Sonia was the wife of Sergei, making her Sonia Sergeiovna Kakovitch from then on. The last name Kaku was slightly transformed into the son of Kaku, or Kakovitch. Sonia and Sergei moved to Kiev. Sergei had learned the trade of making galoshes and was selling them in Kiev, Moscow, and Leningrad. Being an entrepreneur during the reign of Stalin was very dangerous, especially for a young family. Sergei and Sonia had their first child, a girl, Parida, which comes from the Assyrian "Pardissa," or Paradis. In the Assyrian language, the letter "f" does not exist. In many other languages, such as Persian, Parida becomes Farida, or Farideh. Soon Parida became simply Rida, or Rita. Young Sergei and Sonia were able to purchase a house in the center of Kiev. Life was far from being easy for most of the Kiev's population. Food was becoming more and more scarce. Nikolai Jezjov's secret police, which later on became Lavrenty Beria's NKVD, were everywhere. Sergei was questioned constantly. Galoshes were needed in a country like Russia. They were inexpensive and affordable for most. It was a catch-22. Should a young entrepreneur providing goods for the population be arrested or left alone, at least for the time being?

The clouds of fear were everywhere. Europe was unstable and appeared to follow National Socialism. In fascist Italy, Mussolini and his "black shirts" were on the rise. In Nazi Germany, Hitler and his "brown shirts" were a step behind. Stalin wasn't going to play second fiddle to his little Western dictators. In the Soviet Union, Communism was to overrule. After all, Stalin's killing machine had already decimated a good portion of the Soviet citizens. His paranoid NKVD saw enemies everywhere. No one deserved to live if they did not understand Stalin's new order, including Stalin's own wife.

Who was young Sergei to even walk in the shadow of such a great skull collector? Sergei was trapped between providing for his family and waiting in line for bread. Sonia would take Rita, who was only few months old, and go and wait in line for hours like everybody else. It is one thing to have a bit more money than some, and another thing to have food! The political noose was tightening. More and more the tension was overwhelming. Sonia knew what hunger meant. She could afford to purchase a bit more than most and share extras with neighbors who were less fortunate.

The NKVD would walk the lines, and make sure that they were somehow visible. Intimidation was a tactic used to show that many will be arrested, even though innocent, as long as one among them was guilty. The lives of many for the crime of one. In this way, people developed a sense of guilt by association with an invisible criminal. Who among them was the one? Ironically, the population developed a feeling of solidarity with Stalin and his killing machine, fighting the invisible invaders who were none other than themselves. It is a twist in the wiring of most brains. Simplicity is what most desire, not complexities.

Russia

In 1932, the collectivization of Kazakhstan failed and the famine that followed killed one million people. In 1933, the collectivization of Ukraine also failed and the famine that followed killed five million people. Sergei and Sonia, still living in Kiev, had their second child, a boy named Ivan. This being 1933, Sonia was only 18 years old. Sergei was 28, and still making galoshes in fear, traveling and selling them in the open market and making sure that all was legal. Many of Kiev's NKVD would buy their galoshes from Sergei (at a half price of course). Sergei had survived on scraps of food for many years during his march toward Russia, but seeing people hungry and starving all around him in Ukraine was unbearable. He was a father and a provider now, not a 9- or 13-year-old boy with responsibility for only one life. He had to manage to support four lives. Any economist knows a 400 percent increase in any supply is catastrophic, but life is not just any demand. Hungry children cry; they can't understand that a leader or a regime is the cause of their hunger. They can't comprehend that one must have money to purchase food. This planet produces all of it, isn't it possible to just go and take it?

In 1934, Stalin's main advisor, Sergei Kirov, was assassinated and 2.5 million Soviets were arrested, out of which 700,000 were executed. This was the year that Sergei was not given the permit to sell in either Moscow or Leningrad. He was still allowed to make and sell galoshes in an open market, at least for the time being, in Kiev only. Sonia's motherly sense that something bad was to happen was on the alert.

Starvation is living cells eating other living cells of the same body, very much like a civil war or national revolution where family members kill one another. How could any civil society bring itself to that level of misuse? How could millions of people allow so few to control their destiny and lives? How many times should such acts be tolerated by so many people in so many places, on a tiny planet that is practically invisible only a small percent of one light-year away?

In the Name of Life

By December 1st of 1934 the purge began. It was designed to remove dissenters from the Communist Party and prosecute counter-revolutionary citizens as "enemies of the people and the state." The Chechen-Ingush Autonomous Soviet Socialist Republic was established and was part of the Soviet Union. By 1936 a rehearsal for World War II was performed under the title of the Spanish Civil War. The purpose of the intervention of Nazi Germany, Fascist Italy, and the Communist Soviet Union was to show the use of their new weapons and military tactics. The government Loyalists were supported by the Communists. The right-wing rebels were supported by the Roman Catholic Church and Germany and Italy. Between 400,000 to 1 million people were killed. Paranoia was at its apogee in 1937 and Trotsky called for the overthrow of Stalin in 1937. Three years later, in 1940, he was assassinated in Mexico City. In that same year, 1937, Stalin orders the execution of eight army leaders. Soon later, in 1938, he makes Lavrenty Beria the head of the Russian secret police, also known as NKVD. NKVD started collecting people from all over the Soviet Union, especially from Ukraine.

NKVD mostly came around midnight. They knocked on Sergei and Sonia's door as hard as they could with their fists, to make sure that all the neighbors heard the midnight raid arrest. This act was incredibly scary and mind-shattering to most, especially those who wondered who would be next. This was in August of 1939, just a few days after the Nazi-Soviet Pact of August 23, 1939. Sonia was 24, Sergei 34, Rita 9, and Ivan 6. The two children immediately grabbed their father, screaming and crying. Sonia begged the officers to let her husband go. The neighbors came out in a shock and waited by their doors. Lives were shattered. What were a young mother and her two young children to do? Sergei was the family's structural support and main provider. Sonia begged the officers on her knees, saying "the winter is coming..." The officers responded with "don't worry, it's only a short interrogation and he will be back soon..." One of the officers insisted that Sonia go to the next room. She resisted. He pushed her in and closed the door. Quietly, in a panic, he said "give me warm clothing and some food quickly. They are lying; he is not coming back home." Then he returned back to his NKVD tone of voice, "move, your husband is an enemy of the people." Sergei was taken. Sonia and the children waited by the door crying. A few moments later they were joined by members of their neighborhood, most in tears. A few hours after the arrest, as Sonia and her two children were sobbing in the bedroom, there was a knock on the window. Two figures stood at the window and offered a few loaves of fresh bread and butter. It was the NKVD officer who pushed Sonia into the room and his wife. They were both in tears, and the officer said "we also have young children."

On September 17, 1939, the Soviet Union attacked Poland, just two weeks after Nazi Germany launched its assault. By September 30th, Germany and the Soviet Union agreed to partition Poland. In October of that same year, Sonia was asked to evacuate her house. She moved into the cold and damp basement of a neighbor. It was a very small and dark room with almost no heat. The winter of 1939 was to have its onslaught on Russia again. The neighbor did not want rent from Sonia. The house where Sonia and Sergei lived was now occupied by a Red Army Colonel. From time to time, the Colonel's wife would take a pot of borsch to Sonia in secret. With the help of a few neighbors, Sonia constructed a shoe-shine box and began to shine shoes in the streets of Kiev during the cold months of November and December in 1939.

Sergei was in NKVD's Kiev political prison. The initial accusations were that he had betrayed the Soviet Union by being a spy for Nazi Germany. Even the NKVD did not believe that, which was why they started a second interrogation. Sergei was beaten during every interrogation into naming his other accomplices. Each time, he answered, "I know of only two." When interrogators asked, "who are they?" Sergei repeatedly answered, "Hitler and Stalin." More beatings followed. The key to survival was not to sign an admission. NKVD had to have a signed admission of guilt before they could easily execute their prisoners. They feared for their own lives if they failed to follow the rules. Their necks could be next on the chopping block. Sergei refused to sign an admission of guilt. Whenever allowed, Sonia would scrape together enough food and buy cigarettes to take to Sergei.

The propaganda machine was fully at work and people were told about the great accomplishments in the political arena. For instance, in 1940 the Soviet Union and Iran signed an improved agreement concerning the Caspian Sea. By February of 1940, Sonia was told she could not visit her husband anymore. When she insisted to be allowed to see a higher-up Commissar of the Communist Party, she was told that Sergei had been executed. The winds of war were blowing over the Soviet Union. Again, the young mother and her two children were trapped in the turbulence of inhumanity.

In the cold and wet March of 1940, Sonia was sitting in the streets of Kiev with her shoe shine box and two children. The family was having their supper, which was some bread and salty pork fat (sala). A man approached them. The man gently caressed the two children and gave them each a warm piroshky. He said quietly, "Daragaya, Sonia Sergeiovna, Sergei is alive somewhere in Siberia, not too far from the Northern Kazakhstan, around Akmolensk. If I were you, I would head to Siberia. The war is coming and you won't be able to survive here." Sonia did not waste any time. She had but a few suitcases. Her children were her most valuable assets, and she was not going to lose them. She had been an orphan and would do anything she could to not allow another set of orphans to face life on their own. She was on her way to Siberia with two other families who also had their husbands taken away from them. After a long and a totally exhausting journey of almost three months, Sonia reached a Kazakh village just a few miles outside of the Northern Kazakhstan in Siberia. There, she found Sergei.

Not all people have the privilege of taking time in making their decision. Sometimes it is imperative to act, especially when all other options seem to be worse. On March 13, 1941, Hitler issued an edict calling for an invasion of the USSR. On April 3, Churchill warned Stalin of the German invasion. On May 20, 1941, Sonia gave birth to a very tiny baby boy. The birth took place in the barn next to their cow, Maroossa, and their pig, Wassili. The infant was named Thomas, a derivative from the Aramaic Taamas, meaning twins.

In the early hours of June 22, 1941, Nazi divisions, in a surprise assault, made sweeping advances toward Leningrad, Moscow, and Kiev. There was no formal declaration of war. Stalin had refused to believe that Hitler would attack, risking a two-front war. German, Italian, Finnish, Romanian, and Hungarian troops swiftly advanced eastward toward the Soviet Union. The Second World War was in full swing.

EXILE

Siberia

The fact that if we were not born, none of this history would have mattered to us may be incomprehensible. None of the suffering of billions of people would have been known to us. Considering that we are only one sperm out of millions and millions that succeeded in reaching an egg, couldn't that possibly mean that without our birth, nature would have changed this history? Why are we born? Simply to be the carrier of memories? Are we needed to just be a member of the cast in the theater of life? Is it possible that, like our Martian rover, we are used for digging only? We understand that even without our birth, information would be out there somewhere in limbo, but we also understand that with our birth, it attaches itself to us like fine iron dust to a magnet. Perhaps our birth causes us to become a "visible carrier." Without our birth, we may have remained an "invisible carrier."

In the case of a pair of professional tennis players, the exchange of a "visible carrier" is the tennis ball. It creates the moments of action. But the exchange of money, an "invisible carrier," may be the true cause of the game. In some cultures, like that of the Germans, spiritualism and music are very much connected. The music is the "visible carrier" of German emotions, whereas spiritualism is the "invisible carrier." It is an undercurrent of German nature. Germans use the word "Geist" to refer to the invisible, and "Geisteswissenschaft" to the science of the invisible. Germans even have a science that deals with the invisible. Do the Germans know something that others may be missing?

Consider the fact that matter, throughout the cosmos, exchanges a "visible carrier," mostly electromagnetic radiation and photons. And yet, some sort of "Geist carrier," like a graviton, also causes matter to attract. Could the "dark matter" be exchanging a "Geist carrier?" Physics tells us that the "dark matter" exists and that it interacts with visible matter, at least gravitationally. "Geisteswissenschaft" could conceivably be describing the dynamics of "Geist carriers." Could the "visible carrier" and "Geist carrier" interact?

Again, physics tells us that, at least in the cosmos, these two carriers interact to stabilize the universe as we know it. Otherwise the galaxies, through their spinning, would have lost most of their mass.

In Europe, the "visible carriers," Nazis, Fascists, and Communists, had destabilized their world. During the air raid over Kiev, Sergei and Sonia's old house in the center of the city where the Red Army Colonel resided was demolished, unfortunately killing all of its residents. The irony is that Stalin's dictatorial action toward Sergei and his family somehow saved the family from a certain death. However, Stalin's tyrannical act did not save millions and millions of other people.

Sergei had to learn another trade to survive, and perhaps even master it. Sergei had become a tractor and combine mechanic, which was in demand 24 hours a day, 7 days a week, and 365 days a year in Siberia, the reason being that there was only one such machine available for a cluster of villages. In the frigid cold of Siberia, moving parts in either machine or animal had problems functioning. Even in the summer months, Sergei often stayed out in the vast wheat fields of Siberia for days because the combine broke down. The collectivization, even without a war, was disastrous. But now that the Soviet Union was at war, the requirement of sharing produce and food with the government was a question of life and death. The village of Arlovka, in Akmolensk Oblusk, was no different from any other village, as far as the government demands were concerned. They all had to share a major portion of their product with the government. Our cow, Maroussa, was the winner of a medal for producing the most milk among a collection of villages. Believe it or not, cows also get medals. That was her asset. Her liability was that she was a crazy cow. Everyone had to stay away from her when she came back from her feeding as she ran toward Sonia's barn. A few people were known to fly a few feet in the air when they encountered her or made eye contact. When she entered the barn, which was attached the house, Sonia made sure that Tomashka was in her arms so that Maroussa could lick him from head to toe. Well, that would be one way to get a quick shower! Only then, as she put the infant baby on the floor so that Maroossa could see him, could Sonia milk her.

The house and the barn were attached as one single unit. This was done to share the heat. The house was basically one large room with a big Russian brick stove or Ruskaya Pitchku in the middle. For nine months or so the stove was the lifeline of both the inhabitants in the house and the animals in the barn. The fuel for the stove was the cow dung, collected during the summer, spring, and fall. The stove had a long chimney sticking out of it so that when the house was covered and buried under the snow, the smoke could still escape. There was another long chimney over the barn to allow full air circulation across the barn and the house. Refrigeration was no problem. Food wasn't going to spoil for two reasons: there was very little food to go around, and it was very cold. A hollow, dug out space just a few feet below the house but above the permafrost was the best refrigerator anyone could ask for. When this hole in the ground was covered, it was the best place to hide the extra food without letting the official commissars know what the government did not get.

The war was in full swing. Many German soldier prisoners were sent to Siberia as labor with no prepared place for them to live. Perhaps that was Stalin's catch-22: if the families did not invite the prisoners to live with them, they would vanish. It was clear that millions of Soviet soldiers in German camps starved to death. However, humanity somehow finds a few minutes to shine even under the most miserable of times. Sergei and Sonia, knowing that they had extra food hidden, would take in a few prisoners to live with them. In the year 1943, they had taken one Azarbaijani, one Armenian, and one German soldier. The three newcomers, one late evening in November, knowing a harsh winter would set in, went out and slaughtered a government cow. They made it look like the wolves ate her. The punishment for such crime was execution. The Azarbaijani and the Armenian were given life sentences. The German soldier did not believe he would make it out of Russia alive. Somehow, he figured out how taking the risk wasn't that different from not taking it. For months and months, the family of eight and many other villagers feasted on the slaughtered cow. It wasn't that the communist officials did not know about it, they also were among the people who feasted, but it was understood that if you are not caught, "I didn't see it." After all, these officials were also in some sort of exile. Who in the hell volunteers to serve in Siberia? They were the underdogs of the Communist Party, and they knew it.

The killing, hunger, and desperation was everywhere in Europe, especially in Russia. Siberia may be hell, but it is not Dante's worst level. In June of 1944, Rita was 14 years old. She was on the lookout for the family. Other people were hiding stolen wheat kernels in the field to be picked up later on in the night. She pinpointed two large sacks left in the vastness of the fields. A few hours later, in complete secrecy and total darkness of the night, she went and removed the two bags of wheat and dragged them to the road. She could hear the howling of wolves. Sergei and Sonia were petrified, but they knew she had been out before and returned without any harm coming to her, always bringing something home. They had begged her not to do it again, but with Rita, it was to no avail. Who came riding in on a horse-driven carriage but the director of the village, who was a member of the Communist Party that oversaw the management of Arlovka. He couldn't believe his eyes. "Ritashka, what are you doing?" Rita answered, "taking these stolen goods to my family." He helped the child to load the stolen goods and then unloaded them in front of Sergei's house and galloped away, like the charge of Napoleon's Light Brigade, not to be seen by anyone. That act could have meant his execution. That was another of those few minutes of humanity shining through, no matter what. Scavengers know they could get killed trying to take food from other animals, and yet a starving body will make the move. In Siberia, wolves ran away from people.

The seed of humanity is everywhere. Even under the worst of circumstances, there are those who use it. When it comes to children, it is even more so. No heart is a lonely hunter. No hunt is without a heart. Villages like Arlovka are probably the closest places to a cashless society, where the use of money is practically non-existent. What matters are services and guilds. Greed cannot serve a useful purpose. When all energy is guided toward survival, values become prioritized. This could very well be a base on which one could understand life in cryogenic environments. Siberia is far from it. It is only a frozen, but not a barren land. It is not Mars. What *is* frozen is water, but water only freezes at zero-degree Celsius, and the air could reach negative 40 degrees Celsius. Still, that is a far cry from liquid methane or nitrogen. It is all relative and even though Siberia may be a cold place to live, it is still a place where families are raised, food is grown, animals are born, fresh water flows, fields reach great heights, birds fly, children play, and people laugh. Kazakhs laugh, chant, sing and rejoice when one of their loved ones dies. They cry when a child is born. It is not that Siberia is a Godforsaken place, it is what power and corruption have made the place to be. Mankind would be willing to spend billions upon billions of dollars if it could turn Mars into Siberia, where one has air to breath, an electromagnetic field to protect oneself from the killer radiation of the sun, where one could use and drink the life-giving fresh water, where one could raise a family, and where a variety of plants and animals could flourish. By any cosmological standards, a place like that, to any space traveler and cosmonaut immigrant, is almost heaven. How did Siberia become almost hell?

In the midst of winter, Kazakhs would charge with galloping horses to hunt wolves. Their lassos were a long wooden stick (about three meters) with a hoop-like wire contraption used to go around the wolf's neck. When the wolf is hooked, a few more riders soon move into position and add more wire hoops around wolf's neck. The horses fear wolves, but in conditions such as this, they seem to recognize the predicament of the wolf. Animal and man developed an understanding of who is to be the food today. There was a cyclical revolution of prey and predator. The wolves only ate what they needed and the Kazakhs would only hunt what was necessary. One of the Kazakhs' culinary dishes was "Besh Parmak," meaning "five fingers food." It was a delicious mixture of chunks of meat and fresh pasta cooked together. There would be a big pot in the middle of the room. The men would sit in the first circle and the women in the second circle behind them. The men would use their fingers to grab a chunk of meat, bite on it a few times, then pass it back behind them to their wives. This had become one of the favorite dishes at the gatherings of Sergei and Sonia. Simple things in life are the most memorable.

Wrestling was an important sport among the Kazakhs. Toma would go and wrestle with young Kazakhs, get beaten, then run back home crying, "I will grow bigger and stronger, and put them down." He had no problem being trained by an international team of Azarbaijani and Armenians, a well-trained German soldier, Hans, and of course his father Sergei. The next day it was again the same routine, and he would run back home, again promising that someday he would beat them. Thomas reached his third year in 1944. More and more German prisoners were arriving. The Kakovitch family grew to nine. A young German secretary to an officer soon became part of the family. Her name was Ursula. She was only 23-three-years old. Sonia herself was only 29. The young German soldier, Hans, was 25. Rita was 14. Sonia used to say, "I need another woman to help to run a house full of hungry men. Besides, there is something magical about the number 9." Ursula and Sonia used to take the empty wheat sacks and turn them into dresses for the three girls in the household. These sacks were colored by whatever ingenious chemical magic there was. There was no shortage of chemists in the German infantry. A few of them found residence in Arlovka.

There was a German physicist, Victor, who knew more about Babylon and Nineveh and the ancient Assyrian history than Sergei and Sonia could ever have imagined. He would describe the Berlin museum of Pergamon where part of the Ishtar gate of Babylon was brought from the Mesopotamia and installed. Storytelling was the grandest of entertainment. With all of its uncertainties, life must go on. In a practically isolated distant village, humanity had resolved to live together, whereas miles away, they were resolved to kill each other. Sonia and Ursula were like twin sisters; Ursula was like the sister Sonia never knew. Her own twin sister died with her mother Betsy.

Collectivization means everyone must work. The Germans were talented and trained to do a variety of things. Ursula soon became Sergei's combine and tractor apprentice mechanic. Hans and Victor would, among other things, teach mathematics in the evenings and fix old generators that had their own times to start and stop. It was spooky when, after not having any power all day, at two in the morning the generator would suddenly start on its own.

Rita and Ivan were taking extra courses from Hans and Victor. Sonia learned some German; at least some swear words, which would bring laughter to the German community. Slowly but surely, it became noticeable that Ursula was pregnant. A few months later a little baby, Hans, was born. The village looked for any excuse to celebrate. There was a shortage of food, but never vodka. Another cow was presumably eaten by wolves, but the village had one hell of a wedding. Sonia and Sergei threw the wedding and built, with the help of Germans, Kazakhs, Armenians, Russians, and Azarbaijani, an addition to their house that was attached to the other side of the barn. Maroossa was generous enough to produce enough milk for the Kakovitchs', Hans', and even some for the director of the Communist Party of the Arlovka.

Stalin was winning. His purge would be continued. Sergei's name was on the list of those who would be exiled into the depths of Siberia, never to be found again. The list also included a number of members and managers of the Communist Party. Sergei and Sonia must escape again, but where to? Not China, that was too far. Also, there was the danger of an eventual Stalin–Mao cooperation. Again, there was no time to waste. This time the family of five had to make sure that they could feed themselves during their long journey. It was hard to tell who was more often in tears, Sonia or Ursula. Stalin had other plans for the Germans. He was going to absorb them into the Soviet Union, knowing he had at least a good part of Germany. He could eventually make use of some of them in the East, but not until after they had given the Soviet Union their best knowledge.

Wassily, our gorgeous pig, became another domestic animal presumably eaten by Siberian wolves. Every adult resident of the Kakovitch family, including Hans and Ursula, most of the German community of Arlovka, and an Armenian family, Kharatonians, and Kazakhs were generously more than happy to give a helping hand. A decision was made to cross the vastness of Kazakhstan, reach the Caspian Sea, and cross into Iran. Sergei, Sonia, and Ivan would travel always one step ahead, and the 15-year-old Rita and 4-year-old Thomas, a step behind. In this way, the family was separated but only by a day and if any harm came to the family, at least part of them could survive.

One could only imagine the sorrow in the village. There must have been no dry eyes. It is so painful to go through something like this. A written description of such events does not do them justice. Humans are not made of paper. They are made of flesh, blood, and nerves that sense physical and emotional pain. Is there ever enough? How far can any innocent family run from the power-hungry pack of beasts that mean to only destroy? Families carry love and will sacrifice their own lives for each other. The tyrants have none. They agitate the insecurities of others to create a tsunami of confused souls to drown their own. As always, after all the damage is done, the guilty one either commits suicide or runs away, leaving the confused souls and the future generations to pay for their short moment of believing in absurd lies.

Madmen and dogs turn on each other. Yezhov was shot on Stalin's order. Marshal Zhukov arrested Beria, and General Moskalenko gave him his death sentence. This once great NKVD operator fell on his knees and begged for mercy. He was taken away and promptly shot. This time it was Beria's wife and son who were sent to a Siberian labor camp. There is some kind of justice in the universe as there should be. Millions of people were killed by these mad dogs.

Sergei, Sonia, and Ivan left Arlovka the night before. Kharatonian picked up Rita and Thomas in the early hours of June, 1945. They drove away on a single horse-driven wagon. The only memory that stayed with me, and shall remain with me till the end, is of my sister holding me as I turned for the last time and looked at our house disappearing in front of my eyes, full of tears. My sister put her head down and could not look. Kharatonian and Rita were both in tears. I wouldn't wish this on anyone, especially an uprooted 4-year-old child.

IMMIGRATION

Iran

Reza Shah Pahlavi ruled Iran from 1925 to 1941. He was exiled to Johannesburg in South Africa where he died in exile on July 26, 1944. From 1941, the young Mohamed Reza Shah Pahlavi ruled Iran. My family reached Iran in November of 1945. Sonia was a few months pregnant. My youngest brother Shourik was born in Tehran on May 26, 1946. The family had very little of anything, and perhaps was even malnourished. Some of the photographs taken showed Sergei to be but skin and bones. My parents spoke no Farsi and had no money, but we were all alive. That is to be appreciated. Assyrian networking is amazing. They were expecting the arrival of my family. The family was given full living quarters in the house of Michael, a good friend of Sergei who left Kiev in 1935. The city had a large community of Russians, Polish, Azerbaijanies, Armenians, Greeks, Hungarians, and Assyrians. Ethnic communities stayed together, especially where all of these ethnicities spoke Russian. These groups were referred to as Russian immigrants (Mohajer).

In a matter of a few weeks, my parents found a single room to rent. Sergei immediately started the galosh business again. He bought used tire tubes from truck drivers, and like a haberdasher, turned them into galoshes. Of course, not without the help of my mother, sister, and brother who would sit until late at night sanding by hand the pieces of cut tires, gluing them and often assembling the entire shoe. By early morning, the family would have about ten pairs for sale. Sonia and Rita would take the galoshes to the bazaar, while Sergei would go searching for more used tire tubes. In a matter of months, my parents found a house for rent at the center of Tehran (Midaneh Toopkhaneh). My parents had a talent for living in the center of cities, first Kiev, then Tehran. The rent was relatively inexpensive because it was not in the North of Tehran but rather very close to the bazaar, in basically a lower economic sector of Tehran. Six main streets converged at Toopkhaneh, which literally means "canon house." The form of transportation in Tehran was cars, carriages using a single horse (doroshkeh), and of course bikes, both pedal and motorized. The food and produce South of Tehran was delivered by donkeys. North of Tehran was more modern, but from Toopkhaneh down to the bazaar and further toward Shahreh Rey, the houses were mostly single level, many of them built with bricks.

The house initially had, or was built to have, one room on the first floor and a second room on the second floor. The house had a small courtyard, or hayat, with a small (only few inches deep) water fountain, or hoze. The courtyard was walled, a standard in Tehran. The entry door was old and wooden with a good-sized knocker. Next to the house was a tea house (kaveh khaneh), that served Iranian stew (ob-gusht) and tea (chai). Next to that was an Imam Zadeh, a small shrine of worship by Shiites. The reason why the house couldn't be rented (though at the time it was a brand-new home), was that on both ceilings of each room there was a carved plaster cross. The house was owned by a noble Qajar family (shazdeh). The house was said to have a ghost (gen). If the price was right, no one in the family had any concerns. Somehow the family history was such that the harm seemed to have come more from some of the living than the dead.

The rent was 200 tomans per month. At that time, one dollar was about six to seven tomans. The shazdeh would send his servant (gomashteh) to collect the rent on the beginning of each month. The survivor instinct was at work and before long, the house no longer had two rooms but four, due to the ingenious thinking of Sonia and Sergei and the help of some plywood. Each room was divided into two and separated by plywood that had an entry door. In addition to having four rooms, Sergei and some mohajers turned the tiled terrace into another room with a view and large balcony. That made five rooms. The house had a basement that also was transformed into a room. Now, we had a house with three levels and six rooms. In addition to our family, five more immigrant families moved into different rooms. We had a range of 18 to 20 people residing in the house at any given time. One could say that this house was perhaps one of the first commune houses in Tehran. Sonia would collect the rent, if one could call it that. It was based on what each family could afford, somewhere between 10 to 20 tomans per month. Either way, Sonia always paid about 100 tomans per month for our family. There were a few problems. The "gomashteh" must not be allowed to see how many people lived in the house. Just before he would arrive, everyone except Sonia and her children would go and have a cup of tea at the (kaveh khaneh) next door. Another problem was that there were only two toilets. The line for their usage was long and depended on how much vodka was consumed that day. The food consisted of many soup dishes, where almost anyone was welcome to help themselves.

From time to time, educators and psychologists come up with interesting data. There is a claim that a good portion of learning takes place between the ages of four to five. It is believed that the brain has absorbed a large amount of information by these ages. If that is the case, by the time I was six years old my brain must have been numbed. The only language that I spoke was Russian. In Tehran, I heard a completely different language, Farsi. My parents and their friends are now speaking another totally different language, Assyrian (Aramaic) and left it up to Sonia to register me in the French Jesuit kindergarten.

I don't know exactly when I realized that these were different languages. At that age, I had no idea so many people spoke so many different languages. I had reached my seventh year, barely making it to the first grade. In those days, the word "immersion" did not exist. The two programs available were full French and full Farsi. The only thing that these two languages have in common is that both start with the letter "F." I reached my eighth year and by some miracle made it to the second grade. I was almost 9 years old and believed that I was headed for the third grade when I was sent back to repeat the first grade. If this isn't confusing enough, at the end of the second grade, here comes another language—you guessed it—Arabic!

One day, Sonia was called to my school, Saint Louis, and told by the director of the Farsi section that her son was "dumb." Political correctness was only applied to the kids of the nobility, not to the poverty-stricken immigrant, Assyrian-Russian children. Which mother has the heart not to cry, hearing that her child is mentally incapable to go any further? I very well recall the tears in my mother's eyes. I did not understand what was said. Neither was she sure that she had heard the right statement since she barely spoke Farsi herself. My mother and I walked home holding hands. I looked at her and she forced a smile and kissed the front of my head in the street and said "It's all right my son, we love you so much."

In the evening, at our house of many people, the message was already out. My father took me in his lap and kissed me. All of the faces were somber. Women had cooked my favorite dish, pancakes. My mother, with a trembling voice, spoke softly and said "Son, not everyone has to go to school," and choked. I immediately responded with "like Jesus." There was loud laughter. I could not believe the sudden relaxation that descended on me. I was liberated. The stress of so many years was suddenly gone. A heavy burden was removed from my shoulders. Wow! No more school. For the next 50 years I don't have to go to school. Only then did my mind reboot and I realized that I was fluent in four totally different languages. I was truly happy, an event that I believed would never occur again after we left our house in Arlovka. I never believed I could be just a child, like the children that I saw playing in the narrow streets (kucheh) of Tehran. After all, I am "dumb," not much is expected from a "dumb" person, which ushers in a total freedom. I was a child again and perhaps to remain that way forever.

My soul was free, shielded by my "dumbness." I could go anywhere to discover, in secret, all the abnormal events, and go places where intelligent minds wouldn't dare to dwell for the fear of ridicule. I suddenly had become fearless and almost secure. I had an invisible mirror, a "Geist mirror" that reflected back the ridicule that emanated from people's fearful souls. I had discovered the meaning of what Germans may have called "Geist." I recognized that people, young or old, would watch what they said around me, because I would contradict them if they were wrong. Why, you may ask? Because I had a few marbles missing in my head. I was a ghost of "Geisteswissenschaft." And I lived in a house that was supposedly haunted; a house that had crosses on its ceilings, next to an Imam Zadeh. I was the only kid in the block that felt it was all right to be dumb.

I told myself that now I have 50 years of freedom, which is a very long time to a child, and that I should find a task that would occupy my total life. After all, I can never have a family. No one would marry me. I will have no children to play with. I will just have to live with it and accept my eternal loneliness. I am a strange mind in the midst of normal. Not a beast, but just a lamb to be petted and left alone. I am not sick, but staying away just in case, as I might be contagious. After all, freedom is a wishful thing, but total freedom is either divine or devilish. Most people dream of it but never believe they will attain it. Freedom is like a solo flight; you and you alone must ascertain the landing. Freedom is packaged with many layers of responsibilities, some wired to explode in your face. If you desire it, fierce fearlessness and believing in yourself is not the only thing you must develop. The hardest part of reality is control and stability, and for that you must have a steady mind and at least a caring soul. For that is the center of mass which must always stay within a controlled boundary. Stability is the act of continuous management, not so much with respect to the others but yourself.

I decided to count all the stars that were visible in the night's sky of Tehran. I set up a see-through cardboard box with a single pin hole on one side of it. I traced concentric circles around the pin hole. I pointed the pin hole to the North Star and started pinning holes for each star that I saw near the North Star. For two nights, I was the happiest young astronomer. Everyone in our house became curious as to what I was doing. But then again, abnormal people do abnormal things. On the third day, much to the surprise of my mother, the principle director and headmaster of Saint Louis, Pere Le Cunider, drove to our house accompanied by an Assyrian Catholic priest. My mother was shaken. The translation began when Pere Le Cunider said "Madame Kakovitch, Thomas is coming back to school. The director of the Farsi section did not understand that we have a very brilliant young man. He had to learn to speak four languages belonging to four different cultures, none like the others." I must tell you, that was one of the saddest days of my life, for I did not want to go back and become "normal."

I was 12 years old and feeling the warmth of life when the Iranian Coup D'etat, known in Iran as the 28 of Mordad, took place. Toopkhaneh was the center of the activities. The large oval-shaped park-like center, where six major streets of Tehran converged, had a very large fountain pool with six fountains pushing water to some 15 meters high, gushing upward like an upside-down rocket. Toupkhaneh had a bronze statue of the Shah, which was brought down suddenly. The activities at Toopkhaneh, as viewed through the eyes of a 12-year-old kid, had their beginning in an international arena.

In Iran's Persian Gulf City of Abadan, the British built the Abadan oil refinery, which at the time was the world's largest. Mohamad Mosaddegh, the Prime Minister of Iran, sought to audit the documents of the Anglo-Iranian Oil Company (AIOC), a British corporation which today is part of BP, and limit the company's control over Iranian petroleum reserves. AIOC refused, resulting in the Iranian Parliament's (Majlis) vote to nationalize Iran's oil industry. A joint effort between the Winston Churchill and Dwight Eisenhower administrations decided on a regime change and overthrew the democratically-elected Iranian government, even though in previous years the Truman administration had opposed a coup.

Tehran had many mobsters. One of the most feared had their headquarters a short distance from our house. His name and title was "Shaboon Bi Mokh," which translates into "Shaboon without brain." He and some other mobsters were hired by CIA agents, one of whom was Kim Roosevelt, grandson of Theodore and cousin of Franklin, to stage pro-Shah riots. A few hundred people were killed, and just as many or more wounded. The coup took but a few days. Mohamad Mosaddegh was arrested and jailed, then placed under house arrest for the remainder of his life. On August 19th, Mosaddegh was replaced by General Fazlollah Zahedi. His son Ardeshir, or Lion's roar, married the Shah's daughter Shahnaz, whose mother was the Egyptian Princess Fawzia, the sister to King Farouk of Egypt. After the return of the Shah from his short exile, Tehran had added two new names to its streets, Churchill and Eisenhower.

By now, my younger brother Shourik was also attending Saint Louis. It wasn't easy for an immigrant family with little means to send their two children to a private school, and not just any school, a school attended by children of the higher classes and the nobility. It was clear from our outfits that we were poor. And most certainly, did not have a chauffeur driving us to school. We walked. We did not have maids bringing us food. We would walk hurriedly home, eat our lunch, and return to school. I was not a good student. I was analytical and most teachers were just boring to me, not to mention the fact that in a very class-oriented society like Iran, the attitudes of some teachers toward the underclass like us were not good. The front seats in the classroom were reserved. However, I did not care and sat in front, which was forbidden to the children of a lesser-god, and saved for those with means, who from time to time would arrive with a gift, a note, and a smile, and pass it to their teachers. I was quiet and observant, but mostly I absorbed, like a sponge, the injustice. A child's world is more transparent. They are freer. Their relation to the adult world is like a reverse zoo. The adults are actually imprisoned in the cage, and the children are free outside, observing them with curiosity.

In the Name of Life

In middle school, in the 7th grade, I finally reached courses that I enjoyed. I excelled in physics, math, and chemistry. I even managed to pass my Arabic courses, and since I had become an altar boy, my Latin was also progressing, as I was told by the Jesuit priests. One day there was a commotion in our school. The classroom was suddenly occupied by the teachers both from the French and the Farsi sections. On that day, Prince Shahriar Shafig Pahlavi, the son of Shah's twin sister Ashraf Pahlavi and Ahmad Shafig of Egypt, was to begin his education at Saint Louis.

Shahriar was born in Rabat, Morocco, on April 15th, 1945. He was princely and carried himself like his grandfather, Reza Shah Pahlavi. Everyone stood up when he entered with two other people and two Pere's. I was sitting in the front row, probably too tired to stand up, and remained seated. The classroom was mute. Everyone was looking at me. He pointed at my seat and said, "I want this seat" looking at me directly. I remained seated and answered, "this is my seat." There was a deadly silence in the classroom. The director of the Farsi section took a wooden ruler and told me to stand up and extend my hand. My hand was black and blue and had cuts. An example of Deus ex machina, Pere LeCunider and Pere Goyo walked in and stopped the director. I stood erect while everyone in the classroom was shaken by the event. I was expelled for two days. On the third day, I was back and walked straight to my seat where Shahriar was sitting, and said "This is my seat." Shahriar stood up, shook my hand, and said "You are right, this is your seat." From that moment on we were, and have remained, the best of friends. For the next five years we were inseparable, like the Prince and the Pauper. The Prince of Persia, and the Pauper Assyrian-Russian. Two best friends from two different classes, two different religions, two different birth places, but with one common soul.

Shahriar would come stay and eat at our crazy house. I would go stay and eat at Pahlavi's Palaces and Mr. Shafig's houses all around the country. From time to time I would help Azadeh, Shahriar's younger sister, with mathematics. The sciences came easy to me, especially physical science. It was also easy for me to mingle and observe and learn about the geopolitical issues discussed by the politicians and military minds. Shahriar and I would go riding royal horses in the rugged Iranian mountains. One evening, when we were at one of the Princesses' locations, one of the Generals asked me, "Is it true that you go and watch the hangings?" I answered, "Yes."

The hangings took place only a few hundred yards from our house in Toopkhaneh. They began before sunrise, and the body would remain for a few hours for all the people and traffic, including buses loaded with people, to see. People came from everywhere. I could have seen the hangings from our balcony, but I went out to see the reactions of people. I started going out when I was 10 years old, just a few years before the Coup D'etat in Iran. I could not believe the circus-like atmosphere of the event. Some would chant, some would shout, and some would just ignore that a life was being removed. When the Jesuit Peres would ask me, "Why do I go and watch it?" I would answer, "The dying man is looking for someone who shows his sorrow." I would go and stand in front and we would lock eye to eye. Somewhere between the innocence of a child and the end of a life there must be a zone of compassion. The Jesuits would ask me again, "Why?" I would answer, "It seemed like he needed someone to leave his soul with." The Jesuits were extremely curious. They would nervously ask, "Are you collecting souls?" I would respond by saying, "No Mon Pere, just information." As a young man, I felt that my response was an honest truth.

Before the end of the school year, the students were asked to write an essay in French and in a French literary format. I wrote my essay almost at the last moment, because Shourik and I had gone to see the movie "Zarak Khan." I delivered it the next day, thinking nothing of it. I was called in to see Pere Superior Le Cunider, where two Freres and two Peres were sitting around a table waiting for me and Pere Goyo to come in. Needless to say, it looked very official and intimidating. "What in the hell did I do this time," I thought to myself. One of the Frere's began the questioning by saying, "Where did you get this essay from?" and I, with complete honesty and surprise, answered, "My head." "I am going to ask you again," he repeated. Again, without any hesitation, I answered, "My head" and continued, "What's wrong?" Pere Goyo gently said, "We had a long discussion, and some of my brothers believe you copied the essay from Guy de Maupassant, and are asking that you be expelled from school, and forced to repeat the year again." I stood up and in disbelief said, "I have had it with all the miserable excuses and injustices. I told you that it is mine and mine alone. I don't even know who Guy de Maupassant is. If Saint Louis cannot stand the presence of a poor student, then you don't need an excuse, you can just tell me to get out." Pere Goyo defended me by saying, "He is right, where did you think, he could have gotten the essay from? There are no libraries in Tehran where he could go and copy Guy de Maupassant's essay. His parents do not speak French. They barely speak Farsi. Why can't you accept that it is his essay?" Again, one of the Frere's said, "Even I could not come close to writing such an essay in French, and in such a manner." "Thomas, Mon Fils, is it yours?" asked Pere Superior le Cunider. "Absolutely, but why is there such a doubt?" I continued, "In either case, expelled or not, I am now aware of what I wondered about." "What is that?" Pere Goyo asked. "I know I wrote it, but if it is the work of Guy de Maupassant, then it came to me as information, and that is what your whole priesthood is all about isn't it? The question is, is there more to life than meets the eye? This is why you are so concerned. I dropped your own question on your own laps."

College Saint Louis was a mysterious hideout for me. I would dwell there after having finished with my altar services and look at the Virgin Mary's statue. She was always the same—young, invariant, and eternal, but she had no soul. One evening, during our usual conversation between Peres Goyo and Enfant de Coeur, I told Pere Goyo, "I can prove that I am not a soul collector, because if I was I could give one to St. Marie." I did not get a spanking, but was told to write 50 times, "I am never to repeat this again." I agreed and said, "You are Jesuits with good souls." Pere Goyo and Pere Le Cunider smiled, shook their heads, and said, "Don't push your luck," and, continuing with a smile, "Not with us but, with the man above."

My parents were believers, but probably more as a national entity than strict followers of the church. My mother was very spiritual. She would go every Friday and Sunday to kneel in front of the Imam Zadeh next door and pray. To her the place of worship is where her God is. The Imam would come and ask her if she wanted to go inside. She would answer, "If it rains, yes, I am no different than all the good Muslims who pray in the streets." The candles would remain burning till they ran out. The Imam would stop by, have a cup of tea, and give my mother a pack of new candles. There was never any feeling of Christian and Muslim separation. Religion was a two-way street, and full of respect.

Sonia would bake Russian Piroshkies and bring them to the Iranian National Wrestling team at Darol Fonun high school, where they practiced for the Olympics. Takhti was the Olympic World Champion, many times a gold winner. He would come and have tea and Piroshkies at the house. Other times it was "shish kabob," or party time, when some Iranians would hunt wild boars. They would then donate the boar to my family. For the next few days, the neighborhood would smell shish kebob grilled on charcoal. This brought many neighbors into the house. My mother would have bottles upon bottles of homemade red wine. This was Sonia's way of "moon shining," right in the middle of the center of Tehran. Christians had the right to produce wine, perhaps not that openly, and only for their own consumption, but my mother did not understand the rules. Living mostly meant eat and drink when food was available, and the house was blessed and all were welcome. Needless to say, most of the Assyrian women immigrants from Russia were like a Botchka, the Russian term for a barrel. Food and drink were life, and the blessing was, "in the name of life."

Every family has its diversities. We were all independent individuals. Ivan was an eternal revolutionary, and I was a strategic fighter with bursts of temper. Shourik, on the contrary, was more passive. Rita was all of the above. She was 15 years old when we arrived in Iran. She was too old to attend school and aside from that, spoke none of the languages used in Tehran of the time. At the age of 19, after being forced to learn a bit of sewing and dress making, a requirement for most woman if they wanted to get married, she found herself being the first woman to work in public, at the most upscale French-Armenian café in Tehran. Her picture came out in Tehran's most popular newspaper, Keyhan, as "the first woman to work in a public place." My parents were shocked and so was she. She would walk back home in the evenings alone with a brick in her purse. One evening, on Lalezar Street, an Iranian man tried to touch her. That is all that he would remember for a very long time. Rita swung her purse and knocked him out cold. Again, her picture was in Keyhan, "a young Assyrian-Russian girl knocked-out an Iranian man with just one blow." Of course, no one knew what was in her purse. Overnight, she had become the best boxer around. There was a reason for that, namely that the Iranian National Boxing Team consisted mostly of Assyrians and Armenians like George Issa Bek, Emmanuel Agassi, and Izar Ilkhanov. All of them knew Rita and the family. She worked at the place until her 26th birthday when she got married to an American military advisor, Henry Wooster, and moved to the U.S.A. Ivan followed soon. Shourik and I stayed behind.

After Saint Louis, those who passed both the Farsi and the French comprehensive nine-grade exams would attend the again expensive private French-Gymnasium, "Lycee," Razi. The comprehensive exams of the ninth grade French Section were taken at the French Embassy in Tehran. The French Section of the Lycee Razi was the only coed-school in Tehran at the time. Shahriar was in natural sciences and I was in mathematics Riyazi. For the next three years, the core course concentration was in mathematics, physics, and chemistry. At grade 12, a final comprehensive exam would be taken to receive two diplomas, one in French and the other in Farsi. Receiving the French diploma would guarantee our acceptance, tuition free, at most any French University. I was accepted both at l'Universite de Strasbourg and Bordeaux.

Meanwhile, the political instabilities in Tehran were becoming tense. In June of 1963, Ayatollah Khomeini was arrested and put in jail. It was like a repeat of the 28 of Mordad Coup D'etat, and I was watching it all from the same balcony and again had a front-view seat when masses of people from the direction of Bazar marched and reached Toopkhaneh. People chanted for the release of the Ayatollah. The line in the sand was drawn and the government military forces were waiting for them with fully-equipped troops and a few tanks. Many people were killed and wounded. In the afternoon I went out, which was not a smart thing to do. Seeing all the action and not being involved gave me cabin fever. My walk in the street became a march of death. Masses started running when suddenly the person in front of me got a bullet right in his head and fell, causing me to fall on his life-less body, but not before a bullet hit me in the knee, barely miss-ing my knee cap. The stampede of hundreds of people over the dead and wounded bodies, the sound of bullets fired, and espe-cially the roaring of the tanks was enough to make one faint, not to mention bleed profusely.

I woke up not knowing where I was. It was a totally dark, wet, and smelly room. One door was cracked open which let in some light. It was late at night. I was in pain and tried to stand up. I realized that my right foot had swollen and the pain was excruciating. Only then did I realize that I was inside a dark room full of dead bodies. I moved as fast as I could toward the door, pushing at it with all my force. It sprang open and the two young soldiers guarding the gate, seeing a dead man walking, ran for the hills faster than any-thing I could have imagined. I couldn't help but laugh out loud. For just a short time, I had faced a comedy of life and death. I walked to the gravel road of "Karaje" and hitched a ride with a truck driver, who felt sorry for my young soul. He knew all about the unrest in Tehran and the many dead and wounded people. I arrived at Shahriar's house and shortly after, the bullet was removed from my knee by Professor Adle, who was a royal family doctor.

I had reached a point in my life where I knew to thank my parents for their sacrifices. I couldn't thank them enough, but they knew I would always love them to the end of my life, and perhaps even after. My parents, mostly my mother and I, talked a lot about the nature of nature and the science of the unseen, the "Geisteswissenschaft." If there is a future, there will always be more knowledge. We are driven to see a beam of light, no matter how dim at times, that reflects the message of hope. This is wired in our human brains. But the brain is not the totality of the universe. Our brains are neither in control, nor can they even predict the motion of all the electrons in our own body. They are limited to controlling the organs and a bit more. Neural activities are electro-chemosynthesis, and chemistry is only a part of nature. We can't close down the book of knowledge. Yet, like some suggested around 1900, we should shut down the Patent Office. The universe is very intelligent. It is up to us to try to communicate.

In 1962–63, I left my loving parents to try to survive on my own.

EUROPE

France

If one follows the World War II dateline, they realize that the year 1963 was only 18 years after the end of the war. It was current history in Europe. It didn't dawn on me so much in Paris, but it most certainly did in Strasbourg. The city still had not recovered from the ravages of war. I believed that in the West, somehow the war was forgotten. It was very naïve of me. The costs of war were not only the millions upon millions of people who had died, but more so in the injuries that were felt by millions of wounded, both physically and psychologically. The saddest part is that the injured had to be taken care of by the members of their own families. For many years, this was a daily non-stop physical and psychological provision by family members, who themselves had very little to spare. Yes, governments start a war, but at the end of the day, these governments have either vanished or are economically broken. Even if food is available, the emotional stress of the caretaker is elevated to a point of numbness. The joy of living together is gone, and worse, it is replaced by a burden that dissolves everyone's souls.

I realized that in Strasbourg, the war had never ended. Memories are passed on from generation to generation. Even when one tries to forget, suddenly, like a dark cloud, sadness appears and feelings are once more soaked with pain. I observed so many times an elderly person pushing another person in a wheelchair. A person who was once loved is now like a stone, frozen to the past. We are not talking about romanticism or lack of devotion, but of the pure reality of life. There were the mobile and the immobile; two souls in a twisted dance of a harsh journey up the hill of life. One must find and exert all effort to keep going. The other may even be unaware of what it now takes to scale the slopes of life. One wished that all would end soon, while the other still hung on to life. Love should also mean minimizing the struggle of those who loved us once.

Right across the river, there was Khel Germany and the Black Forest. Even flying over the region, one couldn't tell the two countries apart, much less than if they were viewed from space. I would tease my French friends with statements like, "Even the name 'France' comes from Franks, who were Germanic tribes." A few times, as a joke of course, I was told to get out of France. I think this is because sometimes the truth hurts. I meant to understand the nature of man, without which I could not understand my own self.

Strasbourg, at least at that time, was not an impressive town without its Cathedral. However, the University was a historical center of intellect. All one had to do was to look at the name of the scholars that attended the university. Its narrow streets like Le Rue des Juifs were dark and old, reminiscent of the Middle Ages. The single Cathedral tower was most certainly the centerpiece of the city. Alsatians were mostly polite and charming, with the exception of their sudden outbursts of temper. But then again, coming from Paris, that was still passive.

Alsatian names have always made me smile. Jean Claude Gunter was a signpost of Alsace, going back and forth between Germany and France at least few times. But La Place de General Leclerc reminded me that now I was in France, even though I couldn't tell from their accents. The girls were charming, but then so were those who came from the Black Forest, and the Italians... well, I was only 22.

A short lecture was going to be given at the University by nonother than Albert Schweitzer. I established myself at the balcony of the amphitheater at 4 a.m. I had a small cuckoo clock and set it up to wake me up at 6 a.m, two hours before the start of the lecture. One of my Black Forest girlfriends had changed the settings to 8 a.m. This would be the time when good old Albert was going to lecture. All that I remember is the uproar of laughter from hundreds of hungry students just waiting to do silly things. There is nothing worse than a cuckoo clock going off during the lecture of a Nobel Laurate. "Monsieur le cuckoo, descendez ici," was the next thing that made the amphitheater roar again, when Professor Schweitzer pointed at me and ask me to come down and sit in front so that he could see me. He was giggling.

I had managed to find myself a job. It was in the summer time at the Kronenburg beer factory. In the evenings, I picked up the trade of restoring old books. Both jobs were very interesting and paid well for a student's lifestyle. Kronenburg was a site to see. Perhaps every student should try to work in a beer factory. This wasn't just any beer factory, this was a German-French bier factory. You wouldn't believe what beer drinking means till you see Kronenburg at 5 or 6 a.m. Hundreds of men and women would bike their way to the factory. Maybe 10 to 15 minutes later, most would have their one-liter Stein full of hot beer, with two or three cracked eggs poaching inside the Stein. The drinking and working commences simultaneously. Needless to say, shortly after this, most were drunk as a skunk. It was the happiest factory one could imagine in which to work. Each employee would be given four liters of beer to take home. In the afternoon, when the factory would empty, there would be hundreds of swaying bikes on their way home across the Strasbourg streets. I had many of my friends waiting for me to arrive with my four liters of beer. In a short time, I had 10 to 15 liters of beer amassed in my tiny room. It's amazing how many friends one can suddenly have when free beer is available. I would offer my beer for dinners. Yes, I had my dinners paid for before I even got home.

France was in the midst of chaos. First Indo-China, Vietnam, and then Algeria. The French and Algerian-born immigrants were pouring into France, including Strasbourg. Les Pieds Noir, or black feet as they were called, were not welcomed with open arms. General De Gaulle was brought in to create a middle ground between France and Algeria. The French military had many officers and soldiers who were of Algerian descent. After the Diem Bien Foo and the return of Algerian soldiers to their home country, the clashes between the Algerians of European descent, most

In the Name of Life

of whom were Christians, and the Algerian Arabs spilled over into France.

Two years passed. One evening, in a small Bistro in Strasbourg, I was approached by a group of Americans who spoke French and was asked if I would like to go to the U.S.A. I was settled at the university, had means of supporting myself, had many friends, and was fluent in French. Going to America without money, language, or schooling was something I found very hard to swallow. I was offered my air ticket, Icelandic Air, to fly from Luxemburg to New York City and was going to obtain my Permanent Resident Card (at that time called an Alien Card), in only a few hours at the U.S. Embassy at La Place de Concord in Paris. Even my train trip to Paris two-night stay in a hotel were accommodated. If I didn't take advantage of this at the age of 23, I would never have been able to push myself to learn another language. I asked the Americans "…and the reason of such generous offer is?" They gave me an honest answer "You speak fluent French. Plus, you are Russian born. You are studying at a French University. You grew up in Iran. You could pass for many ethnicities around the world. We are going to go to Vietnam after the French defeat in Diem Bien Foo." That was a good and an honest answer. I accepted.

At the U.S. Embassy, at the entry into the waiting room, an unhappy-faced young woman, an embassy employee, in an angry tone of voice asked, "Oui?" I told her I was here to see Mr... and gave my name. Her French wasn't good, and I did not speak a word of English. She glanced at a few pages of paper and, in broken French (translated in English), said, "You must have a physical exam, and you must take your clothing off." I stood motionless and in total shock answered, "Maintenant et ici?" She, still in an angry tone of voice and seemingly very irritated answered, "Oui! Oui!," and repeated "Undress, undress." She pointed toward an open door across the waiting room, where at least 50 men and women and three U.S. Marines were sitting and standing. I nervously had to ask one more time, "Ici?" She, and this time in a yelling tone, answered, "Oui, Oui." I thought, "Oh well, what the hell, different cultures have different ways. This may just be the American way." I undressed and naked, walked across the waiting room where the three Marines were rolling over and laughing their heads off, while most of the others remained in shock. As soon as I reached the room that I was directed to, a doctor and a nurse, who could not control their laughter, said, "No, no, go get your clothing." I couldn't believe this theatrical bureaucracy. I reversed my trajectory, still naked, and waving to the audience with a smile on my face, picked up my clothing and headed back toward the room. By this time, I was told that I was healthy enough, received my Alien Card, and headed toward my next country of residence, the U.S.A.

UNITED STATES OF AMERICA

Washington, D.C.

It was November, 1964, when I arrived at Kennedy Airport in New York City. Johnson was running for President and Vietnam was about to explode. I took the bus to the 42nd street bus stop, but had no money for the bus ticket. Instead, I handed my watch that my father had given me as a fare for the bus ride. The bus driver looked at me, a young man with two suitcases and no language. He waited till everyone got off the bus and handed me back the watch and said, "I truly wish you good luck in America." I thanked him and walked with my two suitcases down 42nd street. The city was just majestic.

It was 7 p.m. and I was starved. I passed a fried chicken place. It looked like a hole in the side street wall, but seemed to be doing pretty good business. The owner was Greek, himself an immigrant, and could immediately recognize a freshly arrived immigrant. He called me and said, "Are you hungry?" I nodded my head. He gave me the best-tasting fried chicken legs and French fries. I finished, and somehow in sign language, explained that I wanted to pay him back by washing his aluminum dishes that he used to serve the fried chicken. He smiled and gave me a job. I worked for 12 hours, until 7 a.m. The next day, I told my boss that I was going to go to Washington, D.C. He gave me a chicken box, 11 dollars, and bought my bus ticket. We separated like two brothers.

This was my entry into the United States of America. I did hope to find Ivan in Washington, but apparently, he had lost his job and moved to Baltimore. Last thing that I knew, he was the director of the Berlitz School of Languages in Baltimore, and also worked at the Voice of America, but he managed to insult his bosses and was fired from both places. I had not many choices, so I went to an employment office, and for a portion of my salary asked for any job that required minimal speaking. A mailman, sorting and delivering mail to patients at a Doctor's Hospital around K and I streets, would do just fine. A hospital meant food, showers, and even a place to sleep. I worked 16 hours a day, seven days a week, for

In the Name of Life

$1.10 per hour. My language improved and I had my job until May, 1965. The director of human services had told my supervisor that he did not want to see a "Rusky" working at the hospital. Apparently, he remembered Khrushchev's shoe-banging act at the United Nations in 1963 during the Cuban Missile crisis. So, what's one more discrimination? I wasn't surprised.

The problem with not speaking the language is that our brain not only has to be rewired to comprehend the vocabulary, but also the slang used by the culture. There is English, and then there is American. My coming to America was to learn the English language. Granted, perhaps I was naïve. I convinced myself that learning to speak English would be another important asset in my language portfolio. I soon learned that there were actually five versions of English, apparently of the same origin, though it's hard to believe. There is English spoken in Great Britain, there is American (not to mention the difference between New England and the South), Australian, Canadian, New Zealander, etc., etc. Then there is the slang, especially in the U.S., used by the different ethnicities. In the 60's, the black men would come past me and salute with their fists up saying the word, "Solid!" I would respond naively, with a straight face and salute, with my fist up, "Liquid!" After their initial shock, they would say "Cool!" and I would respond immediately, "Hot!"

These conversions would not last long; after a strange look, my practicing of the English language in the streets would abruptly come to an end. Another famous expression used at that time and place was, "Say what?" My brain was trying to figure out an answer and I needed to respond quickly. I would answer, "What." They would look at me and respond, "No, you don't answer by saying what." I would look at the person and ask, "Then what am I supposed to say?" He responded, "You don't say anything; you just act surprised." That didn't go too well when I faced the "Say what?" expression again, and acted with my own weird face of surprise. Somehow, slowly but surely, people drifted away from me when I would walk the streets of Washington, D.C., in 1964.

Maine

I would read any scientific article related to mathematics, physics, or astronomy. I registered at Montgomery College in Maryland for the Fall Semester. Before I became involved with Universities, I went to see my sister Rita, in Maine. My nephew, Henry junior, was born in Columbia, South Carolina, and was now about 5 years old. I would take him walking and play with him. I would give him a bath and put him to sleep. Rita and her family lived in Thomaston, where Henry (the father) worked as a guard at the Maine State Prison. He was already retired from the military. Rita worked at Moody's Diner on US-1. She would get home after midnight. The truck drivers would ask, "Rita, where is your husband?" She would answer very naively, "In prison," to which the truckers replied, "We are very sorry Rita."

I was Rita's brother and people wanted to help me. I found a job at the sardine factory. I had to get up at 4 a.m. and listen to the radio announcement saying whether or not the sardine ship would come. Then I would jog the six miles from Thomaston to Rockland to the sardine factory. Except for a few male managers, everyone else was female. The female population insisted that management hire me. They wore blue jeans, boots, and cutting knives, which they mostly kept in their boots. No one, and I mean no one, would mess with these ladies. They could lift weights that some weightlifters would have issues with. But they were the most feminine women, and the swiftest and sweetest. They loved Rita. Almost everyone for miles and miles knew Rita. She was popular not only because she was born in Russia, but also because she was married to Henry Wooster, the War World II veteran and Ranger, as well as a Korean War veteran. But mostly, Henry was known as Butch Wooster, the New England Boxing Champion. Because of the affection the whole town had for Rita, I was hired by the sardine factory. However, I had to lift very heavy containers of sardines and move them, which posed a problem for me. But the "ladies of the sea," as I used to call them, would lift the containers and tell me, "Honey, just stay around and talk to us." The management would say, "Moral is high, keep it up Tom." I made $1.05 per hour and smelled like hell. If you ever want to smell bad for weeks, just try working at a sardine factory. Actually, my blue jeans, when I took them off, stood straight until the next morning when I had to push myself into them, like an astronaut. They were the most oily and smelly pants that I had ever worn—wow!!! As if that wasn't bad enough, the ladies would insist I go and drink beer after work. Seeing us coming, the bar would empty because of the smell, even though most of the men drinking at the bar were the husbands of these ladies. But we were a clan. We were buddies and felt that we were feeding the country and were proud of it—very smelly and very proud.

I went on a few dates until one day I met Jean and her mother Elsa at my sister's house. Charlie and Elsa Kigel, Jean's parents, were first generation American-born Latvians. They had two daughters, Jean and Gale, both of whom were sent to private schools and universities. Jean was a student at Boston University and we started dating.

Charlie had one of the largest hen farming operations in Lincoln County. Sometime later, when I met him, I told him, "Charlie, you seem to have the tallest building in this neighborhood; five stories high with an elevator full of chickens." He had basically built it himself with the help of some neighbors. Charlie was a "HAM" radio operator and would talk across the world with different people of various professions. He was an incredibly talented and handy man. Elsa was a very sweet lady and housewife and believed in mostly homegrown food and vegetables. The Kigels lived on a very large farm in Warren, Maine, with a few hundred acres and a pond. What is a pond in Maine may very well be a lake somewhere else.

Maryland

I returned to Washington to attend Montgomery College. I was still worried about my English, but more so about finding a job that could feed me and shelter me. I had caught the bus from Maine at night and arrived in Washington by 7 a.m. I went to the same place that helped me find my first job at the Doctor's Hospital. A few hours later, I met Steve, a Greek with a carry-out restaurant in North East Washington, on Eastern Avenue near Capitol East. The salary was $1.25 per hour. I told Steve that I needed a place to sleep for a few hours a day but would like to keep the carryout open from 6 p.m. until 6 a.m., at which time he would take over the day shift. I needed my days free to go to college. Steve told me that I did not understand life in America. If the store was open all night there would be robberies. I insisted, and the Eastern Carry Out was open all night. The neighborhood was a food desert after dark. I was relieved that I had food to eat, a place to wash and sleep, and even money to save, and was going to college. The first thing that I would do at Montgomery College was to go take a shower and shave, and take a dive into the swimming pool. I would register every semester for a swimming class to make sure that I had a place to take my shower, but I never learned how to swim. Oh well, nobody is perfect!

To make a long story short, I was only robbed six times at the Eastern Carry Out. The first time was at 2 a.m., just few weeks after I had opened the restaurant. It took some time for the young man, who was my age, to explain to me that he wanted the cash money inside a paper bag. The second time was early in the morning, in July, 1967, at 3 a.m. The air conditioning system was not reliable. I was alone, studying Statics and Dynamics, between two hot pots of chicken and fish stew. A young man walked in and ordered a hot cup of coffee and then pushed his revolver into my face, yelling and cussing. He wanted all the money from the cash register inside a paper bag. I handed him the money and stood silently. He turned around as if he was going to leave but then changed his mind and suddenly turned 180 degrees and threw the hot coffee in my face. This is where cultures clash. He wouldn't have known about my existence and my life struggles. In looking at me, he probably only saw a white man. In the America of the 60's, the country seemed to have been split between black and white. My own family history was much bloodier than the family history of the man who was in the process of robbing me. He could have gone home with the money, but something made him turn around and throw the hot coffee in my face. His judgement was poor. He had no idea of the life that I had lived, much less of the life that my family had lived.

I was like a cornered and wounded animal that had no way of escape, nor a choice to do so. When one runs out of choices, the next thing to come is hopelessness. I was of the latest generation of massacred, exiled, immigrated, shot at, discriminated, and dehumanized living souls. The clash was not between black and white, but between two individuals trapped at a given moment into an envelope of chaos where either one or both of them lose their lives. It was a clash between two cultures in poverty. His neck was under one of the two big chopping knives that I had reached for, and my heart was pressed against the revolver that he was holding. This was the moment where life ends. If he pulled the trigger, he was going to be headless. I could think only of my parents losing their son at the age of 26. At that moment, I had accepted my predicament. Every life must end somewhere; mine would end at a carryout in some dark corner of Washington, D.C.

The police had arrived. My white apron was soaked in blood. We were both taken to the emergency room. I lay down, naked on a cold metal table, as I was being washed down with cold water. The doctors looked at me in total surprise. They asked, "Where is the bullet wound?" I was just as surprised and I responded, "Am I shot?" No. It was the blood from the badly cut neck of the other person. Six months later, in the courthouse, during the trial of the person who had robbed me, he was asked why he did not kill me, and his answer was, "I would have been decapitated." He had shot another store owner two weeks before he was arrested in the Eastern Carry Out robbery. There were four more robberies, but all of them were civil, where I would be politely asked, "Please Mr. Tom, we don't want any problem, just money." After the second robbery, I had two loaded guns under the cash register, exposed for all to see. My given titles were, "Crazy, M.F., Black, Russian, etc." I was one of the community members now.

Overall, life was good. I had a place to sleep, food to eat, a place to clean and shower, and even a place to swim. I was being educated and even had a few girlfriends. One day, a group of young men told me that someone wanted to talk to me. I met the person, who was in the company of few others, in Dupont Circle. The person looked at me and said, "I understand that you are a student in engineering, and work and sleep in the Eastern Carry Out, you barely speak English, you have no one in this city, you cut brothers with knives, and take a walk in a neighborhood where not even a policeman dares to go. What kind of M.F. are you? And by the way, you are dating one of my girlfriends." I answered, "Oh! Ya, which one?" The gang had smiles on their faces. The man said, "Man, you are all right." He continued, "Have you heard of me? I am Stokely Carmichael." I answered, "No idea, but you also seem to have some sort of Caribbean accent. Are you a member of a student movement?" He answered, "I am a student at Howard, but my movement is the Black Power Movement." I did not understand the whole meaning of the meeting, if there even was one. A few days later, the FBI agents had a visit with me. This was a period when "The Black Panthers" were regarded as undesirable and revolutionary. The agents told me, "You had a meeting with someone called Stokely Carmichael, and we're interested to know what he's up to?" I answered, "I don't know what he wanted; maybe he was mad that I had seen his girlfriend a few times." The agents smiled and left, but told me that I should expect a visit from them from time to time.

I was excelling in my Engineering courses. My physics professor at Montgomery College, Dr. Peggy Dixon, told me if I taught the Physics class, then she and the class would teach me English. The deal was sealed, and we were one happy class and the envy of many other professors. Except for one. The English teacher truly disliked me for being what she would refer to as a "Soviet," but she somehow was able to stretch it to "Sovieeett." I guess in the 60's, it was okay to discriminate openly. My classmates, 40 young men and women, were very offended by her attitude toward me. A good number of students were my age, which is old to be in a Junior College. They were Viet Nam veterans. We were perhaps all children of misfortune and did not have the luck of going straight to college after high school. In my case, I had to go to France first to attend the University and then immigrate to the U.S. before I was back in school again. For most of us, life was bumpier than normal. For some, it was much worse; they were killed. I certainly could have been one of them, as there were a number of times I could have been killed. Regardless, we were committed to educate ourselves.

There were many times when my classmates backed me up and argued with our English teacher. She was over 50, unmarried, and saw a Communist behind every tree. One day, she picked on me as usual, pointing and with a nasty tone said, "As a Soviet, you must know that we had our Camelot just a few years ago. Explain to us what you know about our 'Camelot.'" Most of my English came from a French-English dictionary. I wasn't yet at the level where one can dream in that language. Under stress, doing my best to understand her accent, I tried to make up the words and give a logical answer, thinking "What in the hell is Camel Lot?" I responded with a straight face and total honesty, "Camel Lot is where an Arab opens a place to sell Camels." The roaring of the class was heard across the hallway, where the President of the College heard it and came running into the class. The English teacher was furious. She insisted that I should be expelled from the school. I had insulted her. I was in no position to drop the class. I had to finish my two years of schooling and get my Associate's Degree in Pre-Engineering and transfer to the University of Maryland's Aerospace Engineering program. The Associate's Degree would guarantee a full transfer of credits. There were no other English courses; besides, it was April 3rd, and school would end by May 25th. I practically begged the President to be able to remain in class, even though I believed I would get a "D" grade. She furiously responded to the President that I was going to get an "F" and not be able to receive my degree.

Assassination

The next evening around 10.p.m., a commotion started in the street in front of the Carry Out. The Carry Out had a large glass window overlooking Eastern Avenue at North East. I had my Aerodynamics book on the counter and was reading it when a brick shattered the glass window. There were 20 to 30 young men, mostly teenagers, amassing near the shattered window. They had their fists up and were yelling. There was going to be blood in the street. I was totally at a loss. It seemed like a virus of madness had descended on the earth that late evening of April 4th. I closed my book. Much to my own chagrin, I knew I was going to be attacked by a very angry mob, through no fault of my own. But then again, this version of madness seemed to be recycling itself around our lives. I was all alone in the middle of whatever was happening. There was no good reason for anyone to be suddenly killed, but it happened again and again. One instant I was deep in reading about the theory of flight, and the next, my mind was trying to analyze a chaotic situation and I shifted to the mode of war. I picked up the two loaded guns.

It is very strange how suddenly the mind shuts everything else off and all is quiet in the universe of neurons. I was no longer a gentle human, a student, or even a son. It was kill or be killed. It all had come to this. All the years of evolution and spirituality to be a human evaporating under the ambient stress coming from none other than our own species. The human mind can reach a flashing point. The wiring in our brain can overheat and it can all come crashing down. The cause is not important, it's the effect that counts. I couldn't see the young men that I knew so well. They had been transformed into shadows, a remnant of a destructive force. They could have been the people who massacred my family. I did not sense that I was in the year 1968. I identified with someone other than myself; someone who was there standing to protect his family to the end in the year 1915. They moved closer to the shattered window and I lifted my arms of death. I had 12 bullets and two very sharp knives and had even shifted my mind to use hot grease, to be mixed with water and channeled through a metallic funnel toward the attackers. Unfortunately for my attackers, I truly was a scientist. Don't kid yourself; a scientist could, from time to time, become the angel of death. They could be used to murder without remorse and under the name of duty.

It was about 10 p.m. It all could have turned to bloodshed if it wasn't for the sudden arrival of Mr. Jim, running and grabbing his 16-year-old son, "Peewee," as we used to call him, giving him a bloody nose. He made sure everyone heard it and yelled, "Can't you see that Tom is like a cornered animal who would use his weapons to kill a dozen of you? Then I would have to cry the rest of my life for having lost you, when I would rather just beat the hell out of you myself." The young population moved steps backward. Mr. Jim was very well known in the North East neighborhood. He and I used to clean the floors at the Doctor's Hospital in North West D.C. For the past three years, during Thanksgiving, I was invited to join his family and celebrate with them. I knew "Peewee" since he was 13 years old, and had even helped him to do his math homework. I almost killed him under stress, with no alternative left to me. I recognized that there are "black holes" in our lives that suddenly open up and release chaos. No matter how normal one minute may seem to be, one never knows what the next minute could bring.

Mr. Jim walked through the broken and shattered window. I asked him, "Why..., what happened?" He responded, "Martin Luther King, Jr. was assassinated at 9:30 p.m. at the Lorraine Motel in Memphis, Tennessee." Into the night, until April 5th, the riots would continue. Mr. Jim told me, "You are welcome to come and stay with us, since you have no place to go, nor means to get out of the North East." We were considering the options when a black four-door car drove up and four well-dressed black men came out of it and walked toward the Carry Out. Most young men took one step backward. "Tom, you are coming with us," said one of the four men. I looked at Mr. Jim and he signaled, "go." I picked up some food, but no money. The cash register barely had anything in it. Besides, food has priority over money when chaos hits. I was dropped near George Washington University, around 22nd street in North West. I thanked them and asked, "Who are you, FBI?" They answered, "No, brother, we are from New York. You are all-right."

On Friday, April 5th, the White House dispatched 13,600 Federal troops, which included 1,750 members of the D.C. National Guard troops, to assist the D.C. police force. Marines mounted machine guns on the steps of the Capitol and army troops from the 3rd Infantry guarded the White House. Over 200 stores were looted. In the Columbia Heights section, around the intersection of 14th and U streets, a 28-year-old man was killed. Rioting reached within two blocks of the White House before rioters retreated. President Lyndon B. Johnson ordered all the American flags across Federal and District buildings to be flown at half-staff. On April 8th, the city was pacified. Twelve people were killed, 1,097 injured, and thousands arrested. The riots utterly devastated Washington, D.C.'s inner city economy. City residences of all races began their migration toward the suburban areas. On April 11, Johnson signed the Civil Rights Act of 1968.

Further Education

After France came the United States. Despite the "F" in English, I did receive my Associate's Degree. I was in my junior year of Aerospace Engineering at the University of Maryland. I had initially stayed with my friends, Dick Heller and Dan Freedman, and eventually they found a room for me for 60 dollars a month in Tacoma Park, Maryland. Although we were all in the School of Engineering, my two friends switched and donated one of their slide rules, a Pickett and Eckel, to me. At that time, a slide rule cost $100. Without a slide rule, one could not become an engineer. A slide rule does funny things to one's head. It is not digital, it is analogue, and one must develop a sense of magnitude. Is it in billions or decimals?

In 1969, Jean and I got married and moved into a one-bedroom apartment near the University of Maryland, in Hyattsville. Jean was teaching English at Prince George's High School. In the summertime, we would take off and either go to Maine to visit Rita, Elsa, and Charlie, or we would go to Europe. At the end of my senior year, I passed the GRE exam to attend the Graduate School of Engineering, with a very lucrative fellowship. At the time, to earn a Master's degree in Engineering in only two semesters was not common. At the end of my senior year in Aerospace, a research project was announced to a few professors and graduating students. It was of interest to private aerospace companies. It dealt with sonic or supersonic jet noise reduction. The noise level of Concord, SST, was about 110 to 120 decibels. A fellowship and stipend were offered to graduate students who were interested in working on the project. In addition, some lump-sum bonus could also be obtained, if the research were ever successful.

Three Aerospace engineers applied, I was granted the award. The program was part of Environmental Engineering in the department of Civil Engineering. It was to be announced as Noise Pollution and not Super-Sonic Noise Reduction. I designed a nozzle to simulate a jet engine having a Mach-one velocity and the sonic shockwave associated with it. I mixed other shockwaves to bend the shockwave generated by the nozzle. My theory was that if I could bend the sonic shock wave produced by the jet engine, the decibels (pressure wave) would drop. My professors did not agree, but then again, I would receive the stipend, free tuition, and bonus if successful. Actually, I made more money this way than my professors. I believe that if you go to school, you may as well make some money out of it.

During my test, a few professors from different departments who were interested in the noise impact on living creatures, had installed a variety of cages to study different animals, mostly mice, and I believe a rabbit also. I had a compliant, flexibility design to break the shock wave and reduce noise from 120 to lower. I didn't know how much lower. It worked. I was able to drop the noise level from 120 to 85 decibels. That was an incredible drop, considering that decibels are of the logarithmic order. However, I blew out both my eardrums and was knocked unconscious, with blood coming out of both of my ears, even though I had protection. Three years later, I had to go through another ear operation at Holy Cross Hospital in Maryland. Unfortunately, the price of this experiment was heavy. All of God's little creatures were dead at the initial sound level of 120 decibels due to their proximity to the jet nozzle.

JOBS

Washington Technical Institute

By the end of 1971, I had a few job offers, even though the field of aerospace was devastated after the moon landing in 1969. I was hired as a full-time Associate Professor at the newly-established Washington Technical Institute, whose board members were elected by the President of the United States. The faculty were government employees, with 15% TIAA-CREF benefits paid by the Institution. We were, at the time, the highest paid faculty members in the nation. My second job was teaching engineering courses back at Montgomery College. I was also asked to work as an analyst of the Air Pollution studies group with the newly-established EPA, under its first head of operations, Bill Ruckelshaus. Later on, Bill became the acting director of the FBI, and much later Deputy Attorney General of the United States.

Sometimes, there is justice in the universe. One day, as I was sitting in the faculty lunchroom at Montgomery College, having fun talking to my former professor of physics who was now my colleague, I saw the English teacher who gave me an "F" walking in. I meant to be polite and ask her how she was doing. She walked straight toward me, and without any hesitation and in an impolite tone of voice said, "Are you still at this school?" Well, she drew the first blood. I responded, "Yes, you old wicked witch of the West." Man did that make my day! Dr. Peggy Dixon, immediately took over and said, "We are very proud to have Tom as our new faculty member, teaching engineering courses."

University of the District of Columbia

The Washington Technical Institute had become the University of the District of Columbia (UDC). My dear friend and colleague, Dr. Albert Jose Jones and I were each teaching six to seven different courses to make sure that our small department would still be able to graduate its students in time. The department eventually grew large and graduated many students, who were able to find jobs in many fields in different branches of government. Jose had formed a number of clubs so that the inner-city students, who had no chance to experience outings like skiing, scuba diving, or karate, could join in and feel a closeness with nature and people of all walks and races. We had a very successful program. We were both respected and popular professors. We stood by each other and fought administrative and D.C's political issues impacting the University. UDC was treated not as an independent University, but as an agency of the District of Columbia. Jose successfully made it to the position of Provost, despite the bureaucratic barriers.

Our introductory science classes were open to all ages. We had grandmothers in the same classes with students just out of high school. The high school students behaved, seeing a "Granmo" sitting next to them. UDC was a racially mixed school. Our classes would occasionally have 45 to 50 students. Sometimes no seats were available, which of course we would remove some seats from other classes and would hear about it the next day. But what the hell!! Jose and I were people who believed to "do it first and answer later." This, is why we loved our jobs. We each were offered many other positions, both in school and out of it, but decided to stick it together and make the schooling interesting and intellectually challenging.

My introductory courses to the sciences had a syllabus that began with The Big Bang and ended with the major issues of our time. I had students in my class from three generations. I taught their grandparents, their parents, and now them. It was humbling to see the desire they had to learn without fear. Their desire to acquire knowledge was what kept me and Jose going. I created a new version of grading and threw away the archaic method of forcing people to learn through fear. I told my classes on first contact that everyone has a grade of "A," or "100 points," and that it was up to them how many points they want to lose during the semester. This is no different than having a limited budget and watching how one will spend it. I used to warn them that no individual is a government and that they could not function on a "deficit," only on what is available to them, namely "100 points." Just a simple solution such as this, brought the inner-city attrition rate to practically none. The class had become a place of joint interest; a gathering of friends with a father figure who cared. The class was not only a place for the exchange of intellect, but a home. I told them, that they would hear things straight as I saw them or comprehended them through my own experience and education. "You are going to be exposed to the same learning as you would at an Ivy League school. I am not going to waste your or my valuable time on things that you can read on your own. But I will fill up the blackboard with equations, then you can come or even stay after the class to take the notes." Later on, it became, "Just use your iphone and take pictures to download later."

My classes were mostly available in the evenings so that those who worked in the daytime could attend. The students would come after work with less energy and leave smiling with more energy than the started with. By the end of the semester, I felt sad seeing the family dispersing. I would stand in silence and look at my class, with so many beautiful people. With a somber tone, I would say, "God knows I will miss you." Not a semester passed where the class was not in tears before leaving. One by one, we hugged and said good bye.

Visitation

In the summer of 1972, my parents came for a short visit. This was the first time that they had visited the U.S. Jean picked them up from Kennedy Airport in New York. We had a Volkswagen Bug. I have no idea how Jean managed to have my parents, herself, and Henry laying down in the back of the VW Bug, crushed between the window and the luggage. It was something out of a circus. My mother alone would have been a task, but putting everything else inside a small space like that made the Gemini astronaut's cabin look good. But she managed, and drove all the way back home in one piece. Ivan lived in D.C. at the time.

Jean and I had purchased two lots on an Island in Maine, each having 200 feet of oceanfront. My parents enjoyed their trip, especially to Maine. Charley, Jean's father, was an expert in grilling chicken barbecue. In 1975, Jean and I had also purchased a beautiful house overlooking the ocean, in Back Cove Waldoboro. Charley had managed to purchase and fix an ocean-going lobster boat, and moored it in front of the house. Rita and her family were living in Thomaston. Shourik had come to the U.S. but returned back to Strasbourg University and later went back to continue his studies at Tehran University.

The following year, Jean and I visited Minorca, Spain, and purchased a condominium with a large terrace overlooking the Mediterranean. We also purchased two houses in Rockville, Maryland. I believed in investing in real estate. We were purchasing many properties from Maryland, to Maine, to Spain. At times, the payments were high, and balancing the budget wasn't easy. But it was still a safe investment; one that would pay off in the long run. Plus, it was a forced saving. After all, we were both young, healthy, and employed.

I remember one dinner, when Charley had proudly caught a few fresh lobsters and Jean steamed them and put them in front of my parents. The lobsters were big and red and filled the whole plate. Looking at the lobster, my father gently gestured to me and in Assyrian told me, "My son, these are the largest cockroaches I have ever seen." That solved *that* problem. The next thing, we switched to German sausages.

I was always willing to help my country, but not to register as an agent. Signing up was not my cup of tea. Keeping a free mind is what I do best. From time to time, helping would be my pleasure, and analysis came easy to me. I would give my opinions about certain matters and leave it up to the professionals to make up their minds. The war in Viet Nam had finally come to an end, but many other battle grounds were to open up. People with language skills, and technical professions, and who had lived in different cultures, were in high demand. My offer was that one was welcome to come and see me in a café, but I was not going to see you in your agencies. I believe the best way to operate, if one can, is in plain view. This takes a lot of discipline and assurance and self-confidence. Even though my father was arrested and exiled without having committed any offense, my personal approach was that, when no legal rules are broken, intimidation by any one agency or country will require a lot of national or international effort.

INTERNATIONAL AFFAIRS

Krakow, Poland

The year was 1975 and two institutions, NATO and the WARSAW PACT were at each other's throats. At other times they tried to talk. When two opposing nations are trying to connect but don't know how to do that harmlessly, they come up with things like ping pong ambassadors or other such nonsense. Gerald Ford became President after Richard Nixon's impeachment and his eventual resignation. Henry Kissinger was the secretary of State. GT-70 was a group of 25 faculty members from across the U.S., selected to go to the Yagellonsky University in Krakow, Poland to learn about the Polish Culture and history. This group of faculty members were carefully picked to represent American diversity. I was one of the faculty members. There were three women—two white, one Afro-American, one Catholic Priest, and the remaining men were from midwestern U.S. We were to arrive in July and leave by the end of August. My teaching assignment and semester ended on May 15th. I had a long wait, as Jean's school did not end until around June 20th. I had just enough time, without announcing it to anyone, to go to Iran and get back in time. Knowing that Shahriar and I were going to meet, one of the Iranian Generals, and the father of one of my friends, requested that I purchase a car and drive it to the border of Iran and Turkey in Bazergan. There, he would take delivery of the car and pay for it in full. I had the right to take a car to Iran, duty free, each time that I attained a degree from an accredited university. The Shah wanted to attract young, educated Iranians and that was one way to do it. I purchased a brand new white four-door Chevrolet with air conditioning. I financed it, just like buying any other car. A few months of payment would be small compared to the price of $13,000 that I would collect from the General. I intentionally purchased the car in Washington, D.C., with a Washington vanity-tag that read "CCCP-1."

I also purchased two small flags to go on each side of my car, one U.S. and the other Soviet. The car was shipped to Rotterdam and

In the Name of Life

driven through Eastern Europe. Shahriar made sure that I had an Iranian Imperial Diplomatic Passport. The Soviet Embassy in Washington gave me a transit visa if I chose to pass through Russia, stamped, "CCCP." In addition, I still had my U.S. passport. All throughout the Eastern Block, military or police officials would stand and salute as my car passed through.

In Sofia, Bulgaria, I reached my luxurious hotel and handed my official looking CCCP-1 car to the valet. I had no idea that it was a day of ceremony, and the Bulgarian President and some other officials were shaking the hand of the incoming and well-dressed invited guests. I had a reservation at the hotel, but no one told me about the President being there that day. I naturally walked in and shook hands, and in Russian, congratulated the president and apologized for my outfit. He smiled and responded, "We are all working class, comrade." He graciously invited me to join the celebration, which I accepted, and thanked him. It was all unintended.

Not thinking much about the event, I headed to the concierge and asked for a rental black-tie outfit. I noticed a cluster of American diplomatic corps looking at me. Half an hour later, I was all dressed up and ready to go downstairs to join the party. There was a knock on my door. I opened the door and three American diplomats asked If they could have a word with me. I invited them in and before I closed the door one of them said, "Good evening sir, I am the U.S. Ambassador. How in the hell did you do this?" I smiled and responded in a cool manner, "Mr. Ambassador, I am not at liberty to discuss it." The Ambassador was in shock, and responded, "Damnit man, I have the highest security clearance..." I cut him off and continued "I know that Ambassador. I will repeat—I am not at liberty to discuss it." "Can you tell us where you are headed," asked the Ambassador. I answered, "Yes, Iran." "Through Turkey," he asked. "Yes" I replied. "You will drive through Bulgaria and enter Turkey with a car tagged CCCP-1 from Washington, D.C.?" "Yes." "How, may I ask, will you convince the Turks?" "I have an Imperial Iranian Diplomatic Passport." "Are you working for the company?" "I can neither confirm, nor deny sir."

• • •

Krakow, Poland

"Who is going to take the delivery of a car with a CCCP-1 tag in Iran?" "An Iranian General." "What is really going on?" I remained silent. The Ambassador asked, "Before we go down, could you please at least tell us your name?" He smiled and continued, "Or is this also a national security issue?" I smiled and responded, "Thomas Sergeiovitch Kakovitch." All three members of the U.S. embassy looked at each other, smiling, "You are also Russian?" asked the Ambassador. I nodded and continued, "Of course—Russian-American." By this time, all three were giggling and again the Ambassador asked, "Where are you going after Iran may I ask?" I responded, "Krakow Poland." The next thing I heard was, "Shit... there is something going on in some wild wings of Langley."

I did deliver the car to the General, but not before I had crossed all the territories in which my parents had lost everything just about 60 years ago.

Initially, the Krakow mission was a fiasco. A few days after we settled into the graduate apartments of the Jagiellonian University, our Texan faculty member went missing in action. We were to have our name tags at all times and above them, written in Polish, read VIP. We were on the news. Henry Kissinger and Gerry Ford were to visit Poland within weeks. The Polish faculty was basically divided in three groups, Polish Secret Service Officers, the Soviet KGB, and honest-to-goodness faculty members. It was easy to separate the faculty members from the agents. They were quiet and would only begin speaking, very professionally, after a few others, who made no sense, had finished their lecture. The next day, some Polish officials were very upset to discover that one of the American faculty members was not at the meetings and was nowhere to be found on the campus. I was the faculty member trusted by both sides and became, unofficially, the spokesperson of the group. I assured my counterpart officials that our colleague had most probably disappeared with a Polish woman and would reappear soon, the reason being that each faculty member received a $100 stipend a week for pocket money. There was a "dollar" store in Krakow where one could purchase western made items using only dollars. I knew my colleague would run out of dollars and his beloved Polish girlfriend would dump him five minutes later. Sure enough, our colleague was back by the third day, totally heartbroken, and was send back to U.S. on the next flight out.

My analysis was right and I became the man everybody wanted to hang around with, especially my comrades the Soviets and the Poles. I would invite a group of them to have dinner and use cash dollars and my own extra money. A hundred dollars cash would go a long way, even in the best hidden restaurants used only by communist members and high ranking Polish officials. After a drink, they would joke with me and say, "Comrade, we don't want to ever end up where you were born, and please tell your loud Americans to stop saying bad things about Poland and Russia, because you are all monitored 24/7. Each time something derogatory is said, we have to write pages upon pages of documents for the record, and we hate that." Of course, I knew full well that every room was monitored in our graduate dorms. We would gather in the lobby and talk. Poland was the best host and tried as much as possible to accommodate us. But we still had those who would complain.

One issue happened to deal with milk. The university made sure that the milk was boiled, cooled, and then served cold. Some of my colleagues complained that it did not taste the same as home. The Poles monitored all of that and were truly irritated knowing that most Poles did not have the same privileges that we had. We also had some who wanted McDonald's. We were served breakfast at 7:00 a.m. Over a discussion between two faculty members, one said, "It is hard to find McDonalds in Russia." I said, "You are not in Russia, this is Poland." He answered, "I know, it is a State of Russia." I said, "No, this is like Mexico, a sovereign nation and not like New Mexico, a State." Our colleagues from both sides started laughing, especially the agents. One evening, our colleague, the Catholic Priest, was delivered to us, drunk, by the Krakow police. We were the wild bunch to say the least. It was a very interesting interaction between cultures. But then again, we were in Poland to intermingle and learn a little bit about each other. This was a geopolitical affair, and as long as we respected each other's philosophies, the rest did not matter. Naiveté was not on any one side alone. There were just as many devoted Communists as Capitalists. In a forest, trees grow and trees fall, and what remains is the soil, until it also is blown away. Silence and body language was like the soil. We did not have to say it to understand it. We sensed it and our body language recorded it. A smile, just a simple smile, at the right moment, is a sign and it is registered. I loved their souls. I sensed their pain. This is why it worked. They felt my emotions and my wordless understanding.

I was interested in the churches and cathedrals. Poland had a very strong Catholic population, even under the Communist regime. Obviously, there was tension between the State and the Church. One day, a young priest came and asked me if I was interested in seeing a church in the easternmost district of Krakow. He openly told me that the Polish security service had told him that I was one person they could show the churches to. A week before, a team of two Polish secret service and two KGB members had taken me to see the Lenin shipyard, in Gdansk. Being an engineer, I had great admiration for the heavy industry. While driving, I said, "Gdansk shipyard may be a gate that opened to either hell or heaven." We understood the humor that one needs to develop under an autocratic regime.

No matter what, we were humans, and we would either develop a sense of amusement, or be crushed by the everyday tension of a strict governance. We are the soil. It all depends on how much moisture and flexibility the soil can absorb. If there is an excess of moisture, the tree falls. A lack of moisture, and the tree extends its roots and grips. At the Lenin shipyard, I heard the name Lech Walesa few times and when I asked about him, the response was simply, "He is an electrician who is trying to organize a movement."

In the Name of Life

My hosts in Krakow had my portfolio and knew about my family history. A child born into exile, not just any exile, but perhaps the worst at the time; Siberia. Even the Polish Ambassador in Washington was taken by the fact that one of the faculty members going to Jagiellonian University was Siberian born.

The next day, the young priest and a driver picked me up at Jagiellonian University and we drove toward Nowa Huta, but not before we picked the archbishop up at his residency. I was told that his eminence also would be driving with us and was very interested to speak to the science faculty member from the U.S. who had attended French Jesuit School in Tehran, was born in Siberia, and who, strangely enough, spoke the language of Christ. I was extremely pleased. Of course I knew of Karol Wojtyla, the archbishop of Krakow. Most everyone was speaking of him and his effort to help to build Arka Pana Nowa Huta Cathedral. At the time the archbishop was working on enlarging the makeshift chapel. It was a tense moment between Catholicism and Communism. As it happened, the archbishop also attended Krakow's Jagiellonian University. He was very down to earth and intellectual, speaking a few languages. He also had a good sense of humor.

We had a good conversation. He admired the sciences, but the best conversation, though, was the discussion we had about the word "Messiah." In Assyrian (Aramaic), Yushia Meshikha is Jesus, the Messiah. But Meshikha also means "measured," whereas Meshkha means "oil." The closeness of these two words "Meshikha" and "Meshkha" is what amazed Karol Wojtyla.

It was a good distance to drive. There were four of us in the car—the driver, the young priest, the archbishop, and myself. The archbishop said, "I know you also lived in Iran and attended French Jesuit School." Smiling, he continued, "Do you know your altar boy's Latin?" I started, "Peromnia Secular Seculurum Pax Dominum Vobiscum Et Cum Spirit Tutum, Mea Culpa, Mea Culpa, Mea Maxima Culpa, Amen." The car was full of laughter. There was a

Krakow, Poland

moment of silence. The archbishop was somewhat tense; perhaps the shaking of the car was a bit too bothersome. We stopped for a short while, then moved again.

Karol Wojtyla asked, "What do you think is happening with the Muslim movement around the Soviet borders?" I answered, "My analysis tells me that the West is trying to create conditions to revive the Islamic movement in the Soviet Union, from Uzbekistan to Tajikistan to Turkmenistan and perhaps all the Istans. Basically, it is an Islamic movement against the Soviet Union, backed by Saudi money and Pakistani Madras." In a somber voice, he said, "Using religion is very dangerous." He looked at me and said, "I feel your honesty." I thanked him. He was hesitant but I sensed he wanted to ask something. "Are you an analyst?" I smiled and answered, "Not for any government, Your Eminence, just for my own protection. We have been harmed." He understood and nodded. He asked, "What is your prognosis for Poland?" I responded, "My personal view is that the West may attempt to move against the Soviets by using Catholicism. The Union Trade Movement in Gdansk may just be the beginning." He truly was surprised, and said, "What are you saying?" I replied, "Again, it is my analysis, but if the Cardinals in Rome did not elect a Roman Pope after four hundred years, then it will have to be you, Your Eminence; you may be the next Pope." The driver put his breaks on, and slowed down enormously. The young priest looked like he had seen a ghost. Wojtyla shook his head and laughed out loud saying, "My dear Tomash, you have been drinking bad vodka." In 1978, Karol Wojtyla became Pope Paul VI.

Geopolitical Entrapment

Jimmy Carter was President of the United States from 1977 to 1981. Some crises that he faced were high inflation and unemployment. The Republicans were attacking him on some of these issues. One of the Republican Congressman from Minnesota, Tom Hagedorn, was on television from time to time battering Carter. Jimmy Carter was successful in some foreign affairs arenas, particularly as a peace broker in the Arab-Israeli conflict. But in Iran, on April 1st, 1979, the monarchy was toppled. In July of 1979, the revolutionaries forced the Shah to disband his government and flee to Egypt. Ayatollah Khomeini installed a militant Islamist government in its place. My brother Shourik was married and employed by the Royal Iranian Air Force to teach the pilots English. He and Swedlana, his wife, lived with my parents. "The Island of stability," as President Carter had once referred to Iran, was no longer that, and political storms were gathering for a downpour. It was a repetition, or a deja vu, as if I was sitting on our balcony in Toopkhane in Tehran again and watching June of 1963, when Ayatollah Khomeini was arrested and put in jail. This time, however, people chanted, "Death to America" and the Islamic Republic of Iran had replaced the monarchy. My family members once more had to abandon all that they had worked for and move. I understand that there is a lizard referred to as the "Jesus lizard" that walks on water as fast as five feet-per-second. It could only walk 15 feet, but that's enough. Perhaps the only thing that counts in life is to stay alive. My parents had to become Jesus lizards and stay alive a bit longer.

Shourik and Swedlana left Iran. They were granted four-year visas to enter the U.S. My father, Sergei, 74 and my mother, Sonia, 64, remained in Tehran. Ivan, Rita, Jean, and I worked on bringing my parents to the U.S. On November 4th, 1979, a group of Iranian students stormed the U.S. Embassy in Tehran, taking more than 60 hostages. This was after President Carter allowed the deposed Shah, who had advanced malignant lymphoma, to come to the

U.S. for treatment. The ABC television network counted each day of the hostage crisis (444), not so much that it was news, but rather its president, Roone Arledge, hoped it would draw viewers away from a more successful NBC late night show, The Tonight Show with Johnny Carson.

Another "black hole" had opened to swallow our lives. It was a geopolitical event, like how a hurricane blows lives away, and how a tornado sucks and destroys all in its path. My family had once more become specks of buoyant dust in random motion, drifting from place to place. Whereas a Brownian motion requires no Visas to float, we humans need permission to move freely across God's blue planet, the only planet we are able to live on. Boundaries are set only on paper; no traces are visible from space. No birds, no animals, not even cockroaches are required to attain permission to cross imaginary boundaries.

Shourik and Swedlana came legally to the U.S. but were stopped and told that they would be deported, not because they didn't have legal visas, but because they had applied for permanent residency while they had legal four-year entry visas. This was unfortunate timing, as Swedlana was a few months pregnant. Judge Shapiro told us on Saturday, a few days before Christmas, that my family members were being deported. I responded, "Where is your sense of humanity, sending this young family back to the lion's den?" The judge responded by telling me, "You are in contempt of court." I answered him, "Your Honor, I will protest anywhere to save my family members, and under any condition." My brother and sister-in-law were deported, but thankfully Jean, Ivan, and I had bought the condominium in Minorca just a few years earlier. It was to become a safe house for my family. Dimitri, their son, was born in Minorca.

The news about Iran was always somber. It was December 7th, 1979. Jean was involved with painting and horse riding. I was working on some scientific problems requested by some agency. I thought I heard something about my friend Sahriar, but I missed it. I knew he was commander of the Persian Gulf fleet of Hovercraft. After the revolution of February, 1979, he stayed in Iran, fighting against the revolutionaries, but in March, 1979, he also fled Iran. He came first to the U.S. Then he joined his family in Paris. On the 14th of November, 1979, he and his sister Azadeh began to organize resistance against the Islamic Republic, Iran Azad. In Iran, Islamic judge Ayatollah Sadeq Khalkhali sentenced, secretly and in absentia, all Pahlavi members to death. That is what I heard that evening—Shahriar was assassinated in Paris. He was shot twice in the head in the Rue Pergolese, just outside of Princess Ashraf's home. He was 34.

In 1980, Senator Edmund Muskie, from Maine, was chosen by President Carter to serve as the 59th Secretary of State. Rita went to his office in Maine and met with him, telling him the family story and predicament of the moment. He always enjoyed talking to Rita. He transmitted a letter to the U.S. Ambassador in Madrid to help the family. Eventually, my family from Minorca reached the U.S., thanks to Senator Muskie. Once more we were together.

Ivan, Jean, and I had a house in Rockville, Maryland. Shourik, Jean, and I purchased another house, also in Rockville. The family moved into one of the houses. Jean and I had a one-bedroom apartment in Silver Springs, Maryland. Ivan had lost his once lucrative business at the Babel School of languages in Hartford, Connecticut. He was living with the family at the house in Rockville. My parents were 75 and 65. Shourik had not found a job yet. Unemployment was high. The interest rates were very high, near 13%. The mortgage payments were stressful. My tenant in the other house lost his job and was behind in his rent. Also, our marriage was not going well. Jean and I divorced. I gave Jean Power of Attorney to apply for our divorce and take anything she wanted. She was extremely fair, and took the properties in Maine. The houses in Rockville and Minorca that were also shared by my brothers stayed with me, with one of the waterfront properties in an Island in Maine. Jean told me during the divorce process that her lawyer, a female, asked her if she could marry me after the divorce. She said ours was the most civil divorce she had ever seen. And why not? If two people come together in love, why should they separate in hate?

ISOLATION

Grand Canyon

The entire family, this time including Rita, moved to Orange County in Southern California, while I stayed on the East Coast in Washington, D.C. I moved into the Rockville house. It is expensive to hold onto various properties and pay a high rate of interest, but precisely for this reason, the house-selling market was low. I was almost 40 years old and in demand by many agencies. I was a bachelor, still jogging six to seven miles a day, and biking during the weekends. I was very active scientifically, but mostly on subjects not open to the public. I was also mentally drained and needed to rejuvenate myself, if at all possible. It was in July when I took a 20-day solo trip to the Grand Canyon, crossing from the North Rim to the South Rim and beyond. I was physically fit. The first few days of being deep in the valley, solo, and looking at the multitudes of colors of different hillsides (at times referred to as Tontos) reflecting the sunlight was hallucinating. This could not have been anywhere else but the beautiful earth. I was beginning to lose myself in nature. As days passed, solitude was no longer my companion but my burden. The heat, lack of water, and eating freeze-dried rice (mixed with a bit of warm water), began to affect me.

By the tenth day or so, there was a scary transformation taking place. I was developing an altered state of mind. Deep in the Grand Canyon, it was dark. Darkness of such magnitude was almost eerie. It felt not like a place but more like a dark, rocky depth where the rocks and their shadows are watching you, as if you hear their whispers. The heat of the day, the cold of the night, and the rattlesnakes and scorpions, were the background of a long-forgotten scene of how humans lived once. Laying down at the bottom of the Grand Canyon at night, seeing a jet plane flying high above, it seemed like an angel was crossing the sky. Cuts and scars decorated my dusty, dirty, and hairy body. My beard, entangled partly in mud, shielded my face from becoming totally burned. I didn't have a sun tan, I had horrific layers of Grand Canyon red dust. I truly did have red skin. In the daytime, I wore slim shorts, was shirtless, and had on thick socks and heavy hiking boots. It must have been over two weeks and I hadn't seen a soul.

That day, I was sitting on the top of a Tonto when I saw four big rafts, each carrying about 15 people, riding down the riverbend. It was strange.

It felt like the Planet of the Apes, except this time the intruders were New Yorkers. I realized what animals might feel when some other animals cross into their territory. The Grand Canyon was my territory. I was the beast. Not exactly the predator, but a playful ram that had to jolt the intruder-prey. I left my backpack and started descending to meet them. This would be the strangest encounter of the ages between a filthy, Neanderthal-looking creature with scars and cuts and a rusted body, and a bunch of clean, well fed, singing homo-sapiens from New York.

I approached them. They formed a cluster like a human shield. I could have been Robinson Crusoe, but wasn't, not in my mind anyway. To the New Yorkers, however, I definitely was a lost man from a forgotten time. I slowly moved my lips, hidden by my bearded face, and said, "I hear you speaking English, what country is this?" Now they were certain this is going to get worse. One of them quietly said, "America?" I responded, "America? Bogie Moy, I am Capitan Kakovitch, Soviet Cosmonaut. My comrades and I have crashed in your country. Please tell your government to send a message to Russia." Just as quickly, I turned around and headed back to disappear into the hills once more. Halfway through my climb, I still had a smile on my face after a long time of being alone. I felt more relaxed for doing a silly thing and my tension was reduced. Any extended seriousness, from time to time, should be balanced by a bit of craziness.

Inspiration

Information dissemination depends on the collected facts. May Day began in Michigan, in 1886, and not in Moscow. The hanging gardens were not in Babylon, they were in Nineveh, 300 miles north. The vacuum of space is not void, it carries energy. Even fusion cannot convert more than 1% of mass into energy. Any 10-kilogram mass can become a big bang and eventually a universe, if only it could reach a temperature of 10 to the 32nd power, or one followed by 32 zeros. Planet earth, even though extremely beautiful, is nothing but a rocky planet. If water did not come to it, the existence of such beauty would have been impossible. Water is a compound formed by two atoms of hydrogen and one atom of oxygen. What could be simpler than that? The atoms of hydrogen and oxygen are everywhere in space. These atoms preceded the solar system. Particles attract each other even when space is expanding. The field of gravity pulls more and more water molecules together, until a massive center of mass begins to collapse on itself and forms a proto sun. At the center of the proto-sun, the pressure increases, and with it, temperature rises. Fusion of four hydrogen atoms produces helium. A thermonuclear furnace is ignited. The water molecule turns into jets of steam being ejected deep into space. The steam and the dust of deep space coalesce and form snow line. The snow line builds colossal snowballs and proto planets. One such planet is the gas giant Jupiter. Galileo observed Jupiter and its moons and removed earth from the center of solar system to the third rock orbiting the sun.

When we examine Einstein's famous equation of $E=mc^2$, no mass which is made of matter can be converted into 100% energy. The only possible way to convert mass into 100% energy is the annihilation of matter and anti-matter. This is where we believe the primordial fire ball, the big bang, for an extremely short period of time, existed in the form of pure radiation. But the universe that we observe today is matter. How come? A drop from 100% radiation, to a lower state, and the excess of matter over anti-matter means that for every "n" particles of anti-matter there were "n+1" particle of matter. After 13.8 billion years, a universe of mostly matter prevailed.

Our universe has lasted 13.8 billion years but has expanded to 90 billion light years. There is a sign of super "inflation," something that might move faster than light when there is 100% radiation, and where no space-time curvature has yet been formed. Radiation today, though, moves with the speed of light. Formation of matter generates ripples in space-time known as gravity, or space-time curvature, which may act like speed bumps. These cause the slowing down of the motion of photons from the super "inflation" era to the present velocity of light. We have discovered that space-time is expanding by means of "dark energy," whereas gravity, with the inclusion of "dark matter," is putting the brakes on expansion. We seem to be living in a "Goldilocks" zone of razor's edge stability, at a tipping point critical density of about five hydrogen atoms per-cubic-meter.

That is science. Faith is something else. God does not need our permission or understanding to exist. God perhaps is existence, both with us and most certainly without us. To plea or bargain with all that is stabilizing nature is a sign of malfunction in the wiring of the brain. But so is not to question the meaning of existence, ours or the universe's. Here we stand on the crossroads of converging self-consciousness and existence. This may just be our own razor-edged tipping point. If we were to remove our self-consciousness, we would find nothing but the pure existence of the past, present, and future. Our fear of death is an illusion of self-awareness. We fear to cross the road which was always there. We crossed it once before, and we call that *birth*. We have our five senses telling us about our present physical entity. The atoms that make up our entity were spread out in space before the formation of our planet. When did we so stubbornly identify with "I?" We are a species made of matter, volume, and density living on a planet of matter that has volume and a specific density. Our solar system moves through space that balances itself on a razor's edge of stability of a critical universal density of only five hydrogen atoms per cubic meter. Somehow, matter is significant and yet only about 5% of it is observable and the remaining is either "dark" energy or "dark matter." Where are we? What are we?

We are neither rocks nor do we have a Godly figure. God forbid. We are neither stupid, nor extremely intelligent. We are evolving and each day learning. And, as of yet, we cannot deny that there is the "invisible." So much so that we are missing about 95% of the "unseen" and hitherto "undetected" universe, which we so pseudo-intellectually call, "the dark matter and dark energy." If we are having a bad dream, it is because of our own lack of modesty and not due to the transparency of the cosmos. That may just be the problem with our understanding, for we erroneously believe that this little speck of material which is us at this time, is alive, exists, and is visible. Whereas the whole expanse of the universe—past, present, and future—is dead, non-existent, and invisible.

Our imagination is a miracle of processing. Just playing with neural networking systems, we realized that we could make a microprocessor mimic reading and repeat what it understood, perhaps even trying to write a logical statement. So far there is no sign of imaginative work, even far less than what a parrot could accomplish. But then again, no one has spent billions upon billions of dollars to see if a parrot's imaginative capabilities exceed that of our futuristic quantum processors.

Somewhere along in our evolution, perhaps in our subconscious, we started our mathematics by counting numbers. Magnitudes became our standards of measurement. For instance, we define a nation's wealth by its GDP. We operate by the use of adding, subtracting, multiplying or dividing. Then we got smarter and developed calculus, where integration is addition, differential is division, and matrix is an operator. We even set up a system in our social structure for magnitudes to communicate a sort of law. For instance, 51% or more means a majority. As such, a majority will have the control. Our freedom suddenly was subject to being controlled by magnitudes. Yes, of course, every citizen is counted, but their addition is what is counted the most. Since every one of us is but a single individual, the magnitude of people became like the ocean that moved the waves. The best an individual could do was to move up and down with the waves. Some became leaders and some homeless.

We entangled our physical existence with the virtual world and measured ourselves by it as if we were two sides of the same coin. Before long we realized that neither the physical nor the virtual could exist on their own. A third "state" was needed. This is where our "state of mind" forged itself into a coin-like object, in interface with both of its sides, the physical and the virtual.

In faith, if the "state of mind" is sought to be divine and is measured to exist in both of its possibilities as "virtual" and "physical," then the trinity coexists as one. It may just be what the word mishikha (measured in Aramaic) was trying to propose. That was what interested the archbishop of Krakow, Karol Wojtyla, when we drove to Nowa Huta together—the "state of mind;" the "physical" and the "virtual" existing in an equilibrium of one. As I will attest before all, what is faith to my mother, and Karol Wojtyla, and others, is science to me. I don't believe we are inquisitive for the sake of just occupying our time, but rather for something by far hitherto unknown and yet mesmerizing; that tickles our brain and incentivizes our "state of mind." I give myself the freedom to separate self from the ocean of populations, and at times dream and think like a child, where no ideas except a child's memory are still intact. I take time from my clogged mind and cleanse it with the purity that once it contained and it arrived with.

Philosophy and Science

Large magnitudes require different means of measurement, something like "sequencing" and "signature." The cosmos deals with large-magnitude measurements, an account of which is not digital. And I am sure there are no mega-super computers in the universe doing the accounting. As observed, the visible cosmos is a web-like fabric, some dimensions of which are large structures extending over one billion light years. Sequencing comes from the fact that any number is a result of many possible "sequences;" for example, a number "2" is $\{(91-89), (1+1), (12/6), ((1/4)*8), etc.\}$. Each set in the parenthesis has a different "signature." No two signatures seem to be the same. This mathematics works not only with "real" numbers but also "complex values." In my development of such mathematics, the computational graphs, using function-generated equations, produced different "signatures" for every "magnitude" described by its "Real" and "Imaginary" coordinates. For instance, the "signature" of two zeros, produced by "magnitudes" of $(1-1=0)$ and $(2-2=0)$, are different. Using "sequencing" and "signature" leads to new physics and technologies.

Even though we are somehow still advancing with our present tools, the resistance to advance further is increasing. If one has decided to scale the Himalayans on a stormy day, simply moving toward Mount Everest is not enough. The availability of the right equipment to survive until reaching the peak could be more important than the tenacity of scaling the mountain. We have chosen to live with science and technology and progressed and multiplied in numbers. We understood that we could provide wealth and health for an ever-increasing and ferocious species. We live on the top of the food chain pyramid and use a high amount of energy. Yet so far, we are not able to narrow the gap between the fed and the hungry. Even if full-blown bloodshed does not occur, a hungry and weak body still can lose its immunity and become an incubator of viruses and microbes. No pharaohs or kings were able to hide themselves from plagues. If we chose to disregard our human kindness, then feeding humanity is not a gesture of benevolence. But just consider the other options.

The difference between philosophy and science is that philosophy is the assimilation of our internal feelings, whereas science is the collection of our external observations. The order in which they follow is important. Philosophy leads. But then again, we have learned in science that the deeper we go, the closer we get to the internal. By the time we analyze a particle, its guts are no longer physical, but mathematical. We are back to square one, a "physical" exterior, a "virtual" mathematically-measured interior, and a "phase of transition between the two." All that is observable existed in the past. By the time we observe or record information, it informs us only of the past. As if from the vacuum of the inner-space of yester-nanoseconds, a latent energy puffs up a "phase transition" that expands and rearranges the order of the past. All that was yester-time is wiped out of existence and rearranged into a new present. Here and now, an extended continuum is born. One should wonder where is all that was our past, all the mass, temperature, charge, time and space? The physical self of our yesterday is no longer attached to the" now." But part of the information, the memory, remained as a sign post of a "phase transition" of our rearranged present.

All of this brings us to understand a new level of physics, technology, and integration. It may be hard for younger people to believe that, in the past, just about 150 years ago, we had no engines except the steam engine. After using for thousands of years biological animals such as a horse, bull, or camel to do the work for us, we discovered we can actually use mechanical devices. Thus, we built systems by integrating many moving parts in them. However, our future view of technologies should be to construct machines in the way that most of nature is constructed. If we look at our own body, or at the stars, they don't have moving parts, but they function based on the fluidity and elasticity of a substance. The stars use hydrogen and helium, while in our body the working fluid is our blood. In a microchip, the moving substance is the electrons. Nature follows its own rules. Why is it that nature needs laws? We don't know yet. Why is it that the speed of light is supposedly unsurpassable? Or that the lowest temperature obtainable is the absolute zero Kelvin, or –460 Fahrenheit? These laws exist. Such is the first law of thermodynamics. It states that no engine can ever reach 100% efficiency. Basically, engines create heat, which is not fully recoverable. Apparently, every system acts like an engine, because all lose heat and deteriorate. In other words, everything grows old and dies. Matter seems to be cursed to decompose. But it seems that is true only for the visible, and not for the invisible "dark matter." Is it possible that the "dark matter" may not emit heat, and if so, then the laws of thermodynamics do not apply to it? Is matter an exception rather than the rule?

Heat is a strange thing. Its effect on materials is roughly of two kinds. Virtually all material expands when heated, and contracts when cooled. An iron rod will expand when hot. Pour water on it and cool it, the expansion reverses to contraction. If observation was the only foundation of science, that would have been simple. There are, however, some exceptions. Exceptions are usually interesting. Water behaves slightly different. Contraction usually means molecules coming together and density increasing. When water is cooled, it contracts into ice, but in this phase, it is less dense. Water molecules rearrange themselves into structures occupying more open space, ice floats. Thus, in its phase transition from a liquid to a solid state, as with ice, it initially looks like the water molecules have expanded during the cooling. Is there anything else that, when cooled, will expand? It seems that the space-time fabric behaves like that. But let's not jump to a quick conclusion. The open space of ice structure is not space-time fabric. Space-time fabric contracts when hot and expands when cold, which is the reverse of what we expect from the material world. Interestingly, the material world and its background behave in reverse with respect to heat. The big bang was very hot, $1.4*10^{32}$ Kelvins, and was an extremely contracted space, roughly 10^{-33}

centimeters, whereas, today's deep space temperature is 2.7 Kelvin and space-time has expanded to at least 10^{28} centimeters and continues to expand. The "dark energy," on the other hand, is explained as the expansion of the universe due to some force which acts against gravity. Is it really? Or is it just a property of the background space-time fabric itself, that will expand if cooled? In short, science is not as simple as one may think and easy and quick conclusions are not always the best to follow.

Occam's razor, in a nut shell, says that the simplest explanation is usually the correct one. Actually, translated it states, "Entities should not be multiplied unnecessarily." Occam's razor was made use of in some important scientific instances. Comparing Einstein's theory of special relativity with Lorentz's theory that rulers contract and clocks slow down when in motion near the speed of light through "ether," a window of possibility was recognized. The realization was that Einstein's equations for transforming space-time are the same as Lorentz's equations of transforming rulers and clocks. Since "ether" could not be detected according to the equations of Lorentz and Maxwell, by Occam's razor it had to be eliminated, (the simplest of competing theories to be preferred to the more complex). In his quantum derivation, even Heisenberg made some use of Occam's razor. It is important to realize that none of these equations predicted "dark matter" or "dark energy," whereas, 95% of the universe seems to contain just that. Should we then simply eliminate the existence of "dark matter" or "dark energy" also? Of course not. The damage done by simplistic explanations and or eliminations of events hitherto unknown to us can be extremely dangerous. Airplanes, such as Airbus or Boeing jumbo jets are not in the realm of simplicity; they fly only because of their complexity. Over 150 years ago, these objects would have been considered the art of witchcraft. Our mind accepts simplicity and rejects complexity. For almost a century, we have been at a standstill with only two major theories, relativity and quantum. Now, we have realized other findings that are unexplained, at least by the special theory of relativity and its insistence that the maximum attainable universal velocity is the speed of light. This is like saying that the maximum attainable velocity for any rocket is the escape velocity, and once it leaves the surface of earth, the rocket is cursed to always follow 11.2 km-per-second for the rest of its trip.

Laws of nature are rule, which impose order on chaos.

Zone Interdit

Systems are often set up to do one thing, but the opposite happens. For instance, the yellow traffic light means "slowdown," but most accelerate. In the roads, we have signs that point either to the "left" or to the "right." These are "sharp" commands. If instead, we had signs that read "please slowly move from the left to the right." That would be a "smooth" request because motion is associated with a smoothness and curvature, versus left or right commands which are sharp angles. This is like comparing part of a circle with a triangle. The binary systems are based on "sharpness," such as "on" or "off." Our legal interrogations are based on sharpness, "yes" or "no," whereas our daily operations are based on a kind of smoothness. We fly millions of people daily, mostly smoothly. We don't operate based on "take off" or "crash."

Somehow, our mind operates between these two different systems. To balance our body mass and to stand erect, we evolved to be bi-pedal "left" or "right." How did we manage to transform the action of "sharpness" for instance, bi-pedal movement, to be controlled by a mind that operates mostly in smoothness? In the language of mathematics, we do have operations that can transform sharpness into smoothness. The question is how much information do we lose during such translation? Choosing one path also means we missed all other possible paths. When we choose, we also introduce uncertainty. In physics, when we chose to observe energy, we will be uncertain about time—Einstein. Or, when we observe momentum we will be uncertain about position—Uncertainty Principle by Heisenberg. If we are set up to do something, we should be aware that the opposite is also part of the possibility.

Science is not a momentary operation. It must operate for all time. Gravity does not exist only on Mondays. It is present all other days of the week too. Today's electronic processors use binary numbers. This is what I call "sharpness," of "one" or "zero." The use of quantum, micro-processors in the future is also being discussed. As long as micro-processors are used, they will operate based on the motion of electrons, electronics. For example, to compile information about probability, we use factorials. If we pick a number at random, such as n=5, its factorial is simply 5!=1*2*3*4*5=120. You can use any calculator and see that 5! Is equal to 120. But now, try the negative value of the same number, n=−5. And use any computer that you want, the negative range does not produce an answer and a major section of mathematics falls short of predicting solutions. Nature answers to both positive and negative values. Dismissing an operation for negative factorials guarantees a lack of information about this zone. It is dangerous for science to work in a "zone interdit."

Think Tank

I was introduced to and joined a group named "The McClean Project." I recognized my lack of knowledge with respect to human sciences. Dr. Robert R. Carkhuff is a renowned psychologist and social scientist. The group included my colleague and good friend Dr. Sabine O'Hara, an economist and agriculturist, graduate of Gottingen University in Germany, and former president of Roanoke College and the director of Fulbright Scholars, also the Dean of the School of Agriculture at the University of the District of Columbia. Other distinguish members are Drs. George and Karen Banks, Hernan Oyarzabal, and Don Benoit. Sabine and I met when she became the Dean of our College at the University of the District of Columbia (UDC). I had been at this institution for about 41 years when Sabine arrived. I knew the politics of the school in general. I sensed that Sabine could become a target. She was hard working, with ethics and the credentials that went with it. After all, she is German. She liked to have closures on different projects. That wasn't the norm at our school. She was impressed with my scholastic work and patents. We decided to write an interdisciplinary book titled, *Physics and the New Economy*. On one of these meetings, in a café in Washington, we were deeply involved in an argument over definitions. Needless to say, we are both bullheaded and stand our ground. Three retired State Department women were watching us, one of whom asked Sabine, "I am detecting a slight accent, may I ask where it is from?" Sabine smiled and answered, "I am German." The same question was posed to me. I answered with a bit more serious tone, "I am Russian." The same person asked, "Where did you two meet?" I banged the table and said, "In Stalingrad!" All five of us roared with laughter.

Every Wednesday night, Bob, Sabine, George, Hernan, Don, and I would meet at the Carkhuff's house and share our views in some aspect of social and human behavior. We had full admiration for Bob's intellectual and scientific endeavors. Bob's view was that "generativity" was primarily a function of the human brain. Sabine and I would argue that the brain was in control of the organs but not in the realm of billions of molecules that exist in our own body. The molecules and the elementary particles in our body do not communicate directly with our brain. They follow their own quantum dynamic rules. Our brain is designed to stabilize our body in the same manner that fly-by wire stabilizes an airplane during its flight but has no control over the atoms of composites or alloys from which the airplane is constructed. Needless to say, when a team of scholars and strong personalities assemble, the ambient environment is charged. We all liked and respected each other, though. Our team's scientific works are recorded in Carkhuff's virtual library of generativity. Our discussions would generally end up in seeking better definitions for parameters used in scientific fields.

Information

The exchange of information is communication. Communication is a miracle, and apparently there is more of it in the universe than previously expected. But what is "information?" The gravity that traps us to our planet is an exchange of gravitons between us and the Earth. If gravity is a form of communication, then a graviton may be considered information. If writing is considered a form of communication, is an alphabet information? What if a monkey used the 26 letters of the English alphabet and filled up pages of printout, would that still be a form of communication, or is comprehension also a factor in communication? Since plants require sunlight, are electromagnetic waves "information?" We have not established the fundamental question about "information." How can we build solid, theoretical propositions on a weak foundation? If we do, the best we would have would be suppositions. And yet, if communication did not exist, a system's stability is at risk. Any disconnect in communication in the system could be harmful. A simple misprint in one of the four compounds of DNA will differ from a previous one and mutate the species.

Consider a tennis match as viewed from space and an alien observer trying to figure out what is happening. The observation would take note that hundreds of people came together from all over, and hours later dissipated and went their own way. At first it seems as if there is an attractive force followed by a repulsive force. The alien is a good physicist and knows that to have any force one needs an "interacting agent," like gravitons. Their interactions will express gravity. Our photons express electromagnetic interactions. What was the "interacting agent" during the tennis match that held the audience together and then released them? The answer is the tennis ball. One single tennis ball. Not billions of tennis balls interacting among the audience, but simply one between two "qualified" players. An important factor that is often missed in human and physical sciences may just be that. What or whom is "qualified" to transmit or receive "interacting agents."

Matter is "qualified" to receive and transmit electromagnetic waves. Matter radiates. "Dark matter" may not radiate, but it still may transmit neutrinos and perhaps both matter and "dark matter" are "qualified" to transmit or receive gravitons.

Dark energy is described as the force that causes the expansion of our universe. Could expansion also be caused by the excess of like charges, or couldn't the property of the space-time fabric itself be that when cooled it will expand? This is only one possibility. Or perhaps the Dark energy is emitting gravitons faster than the speed of light, and we are then not "qualified" to detect them because in our physics we have set up rules that claim that the speed of light is the maximum attainable velocity in the universe, that and any gadget that we build for the detection of gravitons is based on our erroneous assumption. Obviously dark matter and dark energy exist.

Married with Children

In 1982, I met Luba at my parents' house in Rockville, Maryland. I met her again in January of 1983, and by March 20, 1983, we were married. Our son Christopher was born on December 30, 1983, just one day before New Year's Eve, which helped us for tax purposes to be a family of three. Chris was my toy. Children, as far as I am concerned, are and should be treated like toys. It is play time and to hell with everything else. Children need not know about the struggles that parents might face. They did not ask to be born, but if present, they are to be loved and played with unconditionally.

By 1983, all of my other family members had moved to California. Then on April 3, 1987, our sweetheart Natalie was born. The first thing that I did was to take her baby picture and show it to my mother, who was ill. By now, Sergei and Sonia had four grandchildren: Henry, Dimitri, Christopher, and Natalie, with Natalie being the only girl. On Mother's Day, May 7, 1987, just about a month after Natalie's birthday, our mother, Sonia, passed away.

Tell me about life. Are we born to just die? Or do we die to be born? The moment my mother passed away, an instant after she stopped living, she looked exactly like herself, except her hands and body were cold. The body stayed, the heat was gone. Her face looked like a 17-year-old teenage girl, smooth with no wrinkles. She was 72 years of age. A motherless daughter, a wife, a mother, a grandmother, an aunt, and a sister. Being a single mother raising two children, she had suffered a massacre, exile, immigrations, and illness. She had to learn Russian, Assyrian, Farsi, and a bit of English. She had no time with which to get a formal education, yet, on her death bed, she would recite to me Pushkin and Lermontov. She was a poet; not in writing, but in life. She absorbed pain in solitude and translated it into poetry. She held her children in her arms and fed them and sang for them, through cold nights and hot days, with her eyes full of tears. She spread her love like a nutrient so that her children could grow. She told me, "My Son,

I am blessed to die with dry eyes not to have seen my children dying before me." She was a mother like all mothers, who would give her life before letting any harm come to her children.

My mother was dead. My children were born. A balance in the realm of life and death. I found an equilibrium between the memory of my beloved mother and the love of my family and children. Whenever I see children in the street, I just freeze and look at them with a smile and most of the time they return my smile. I sense their presence as a gift, sent to earth from beyond. I shake my head as a salute and they return my salute back with their smile. It is a most interesting interaction. If I knew more about the true definition of information I would swear that we are interchanging information and somehow communicating. How is it possible that such beautiful little creatures could sometime later become the takers of life?

Luba worked at Northrop Grumman. She travelled around the world. Salary-wise, she made more money than I made as an Associate Professor. However, as I would remind her, my contract was only nine months a year, and perhaps 20 hours a week. And, of course, I had two weeks for Christmas and a week for spring break. She would respond, "But you are never home." I would answer, "What's wrong with home being a French café, where they serve chocolate croissants? After Natalie was born, two things happened to Luba: she stopped smoking and she stopped working (at least not at Northrop Grumman but a whole lot more at home without pay). This is the unfortunate true story for most mothers. We even have a name for it, "housewife," as if we also have a "street wife." Social injustices start at home. Imagine if men were to bear a growing embryo in their beer belly, since I don't know where else, for nine months. Perhaps God initially tried it and said, "Oh my God! What a useless species!" Just look at the animal kingdom. Consider the king of the jungle, the lion. He is as lazy as they come, sleeping most of the time, whereas the lionesses go and hunt for the family. Well, I did not sleep but did what most great fathers do, which is to find all the good reasons I can to take my children to any café or doughnut shop and to say, "Thank you God for our daily doughnut." I believed, and still do, that the more you eat, the more you lose weight because the body has to work harder. Luba would say, "If you can prove this, you will be the richest man on earth." I am still working on this theory.

Innovative Discoveries

A professor's salary is not enough to raise two children and live comfortably in Washington, D.C. I always had to expand my income by either buying or selling houses or land. Real estate usually worked in my favor. In one of the real estate meetings, I met Tom Hagedorn, the former Republican Congressman from Minnesota. I had seen him on T.V. arguing with Democrats. I asked him, "Are you an ex-congressman?" He responded, "We don't refer to ourselves as such; it sounds like an ex-con." I responded, "Don't you serve one term in Congress and one term in jail?" We had a good laugh. We became good friends and business partners for years to come. I also continued research that I had started around 1979. I met the President and Vice President of an information technology company in Reston, Virginia. We tested my work in encryption. The FBI was very concerned about some uninvited people who were snooping around and attempting to get closer to me. A few agents had requested to meet with me. I mostly preferred to have meetings at my house. Some people in DOD, DIA, and foreign countries got wind of the encryption. Shortly later, we had documents that were encrypted and decrypted by my newly developed algorithm. The House Intelligence Committee asked me if I could present the encryption to them. NSA was to decode an encrypted message given to them by a U.S. Senator. The meeting took place in the "dungeon" of the U.S. Congress. I don't know if the message was ever decoded. The encryption could have been a lucrative way of producing extra income, but I wasn't interested.

Tom Hagedorn and I bought and sold few properties together. For a short time, we even bought a vacuum shop, just to try the life of a retail shop owner. After a year and half, we gave the shop to one of our employees. In the meantime, I published a scientific paper on saving energy in steam power plants. This was based on a few of my proprietary intellectual properties. I was awarded several patents. These patents and the scientific paper described the potential thermodynamic efficiencies obtainable in a steam power plant. My theory was tested at the United States Naval Academy, and at a power plant in McAllen, Texas. The theory showed both scalability and an increase in efficiency of 2.1% at the USNA, and 3.1% at the McAllen, Texas, power plant for only an insertion of 1/10th of 1% (0.1%) of helium. I traveled around the world presenting the theory and the results of these two tests. I met with a few Ministers of Energy of various countries. The science and the tests proved that increases of 5% to 10% efficiencies were attainable. The technology could have evolved to produce even up to 20% increase in efficiencies in steam power plants if sincerity was the primary incentive.

Royal Family

I was introduced to the Royal Family of Ethiopia, His Majesty Haile Selassie, the Second, and the Empress. Tom Hagedorn and I took the Royal family a few times to the U.S. Senate and met with a few Senators. My family and the Royal family became close friends. The Royal family invited Luba and I to have dinner at their house in Oakton, Virginia. The Emperor graciously asked me to bring a friend of mine. I was accompanied by Dr. Albert Jose Jones and his wife Paula. The Ethiopian food was delicious, especially when cooked by a Royal Princess. The Emperor and Empress liked to have Christopher and Natalie come with us. I used to take the Royal family and the children to have pizza in Tyson's Corner, accompanied by five Rastafarian body guards. The Emperor and the Empress would hold Christopher and Natalie on their laps and enjoy their giggles. It was nice seeing the royal family a bit more relaxed. These were not easy times. The Selassie family lived far away from their beloved country. We had many meetings regarding the geopolitical situation in Ethiopia. Tom Hagedorn and I arranged many meetings with various people. We looked into the availability of many options. The Empress was active and very much involved in all decision-making. She oversaw the daily activities with regard to the Emperor's health, family, and international meetings. Some meetings were held at the Washington Press Club. The Royal family was devoted to their country until the end.

Today, true Royal families are the accidental wealthy. By accidental, I mean if everything else were repeated again, such wealth could not be accumulated by the same people on a second throw of a dice. There will also be more to come since the new wave of reaching beyond royal wealth is just appearing on the horizon. I am certain that "trillionaires" will replace billionaires. It is only a matter of technological advancement. The event of growing wealthy beyond the GDPs of most nations is like a surgical knife that will cut through the social fabric. But, like a surgical knife, it is also a necessary tool to operate. This is like a double-edged sword that could cut on either side. The outcome depends on the population at large.

Perhaps greed is nature's way of pushing a lethargic evolution of mankind into the fast lane. For too long, mankind sat and wasted good nature's time on cutting stones. We had the Old Stone Age, Middle Stone Age, and New Stone Age. Time may be money on earth, but it is energy in the cosmos. We trapped ourselves inside our own psychological black hole, thinking there was nothing outside. Such narcissism, to believe that the cosmos had been exclusively rented to us? We are now finally realizing that we have imprisoned ourselves in a state of mind and not in the reality that is the universe. We are beginning to see our psychological "event horizon" through which we must exit and reach others. Is it even possible to break through, since our theories in physics about black holes claim that not even light could escape the "event horizon?" The answer is yes. How else could the gravitational waves of a black hole be felt outside its "event horizon?" Thus, will civilizations that were once trapped within their own psychological black holes of taboos and fears and lack of technological advancement cross their "event horizon?"

Trillions of dollars of wealth are flying in space with more rare earth and minerals inside them than in some countries. It will take a bit more blood, guts, and perhaps even tears, and few more breakthroughs in physics and engineering, to bring this wealth back to earth. One has to always milk the economy. Economy is not a natural substance but it is of this nature. One can extract it from nature. Economy is an available nutrient that could either make a species grow or poison it beyond repair. Social structures, such as governments, will no longer control the destiny of mankind, companies will. We hope these companies are not run by autocrats or tyrants. We pray that we won't have "Ivan the terrible," but instead "Ivan the beautiful." And why could Ivan not be beautiful, you know. From time to time, a few wealthy people invited me to meet with them. Some meetings took place at the billionaires' yachts, some in their offices, and some in their houses. Their main interest was to talk to someone who had outside-of-the-box ideas and was not afraid of making them known. I guess when money is no longer an option, and mortality is certain, then curiosity prevails.

Life and Family

Our family had grown. Henry met Laura at Yale University and shortly after, they were married. As young newly-graduated students looking for jobs, they moved to Washington, D.C. and lived with us for a while. These were fantastic times. I remember when Henry was a baby, giving him a bath and washing his butt. Now, I was giving a bath to Christopher and Natalie. I taught late classes to save time to do my other research and work during the day. Even at 10 o'clock in the evening, Chris and Natalie were waiting to play soccer in the hallway inside the house. We would start the game and after few goals (always scored by them), they were ready to go to bed. There were many times I broke my big toe playing barefooted late-night soccer in our narrow hallway. Going to bed was always a journey into a long night. I would start with "Once upon a time" and tell them a story. But the next night when I would start again with "Once upon a time..." I would be interrupted by both of them saying, "No! No! We don't want to hear this story," so I would restart and reboot with, "Twice upon a time ..." You can see that that is a different story. It kind of reminded me of politics where it is the same story, but slightly twisted from the beginning.

I was a father like Sergei was. He insisted on living on his own. He lived in Cerritos in Southern California just a few miles from Rita. Ivan lived in the same apartment, but two floors up. Shourik and Swedlana lived in their own house just few miles away. Our father exercised every morning until he was diagnosed with Pancreatic Cancer. He told Rita, "When I no longer am able to walk or exercise, I want to die." Seven days later he stopped walking and went into a coma. A few days later, he passed away. He was 94 years old. Our parents Sonia and Sergei lay side-by-side in the Park Lawn Cemetery in Hollywood. It seems ironic that of all possible places, their graves are located in the fictitious land of Hollywood. Perhaps this was because their real lives were stranger than fiction; two simple people, entangled in a vortex of politics and national struggles, bound by a common string of human desire to survive under any condition. Two orphans through no fault of their own; who had dodged the misfortunes of life. They educated their children while barely making ends meet. They never spoke against any preaching. They found their integrity in simply being parents. This is why when our loved ones die and the realization that they will never walk through the door again sets in, it seems as though they never existed, and yet we know that they did. Our memories of them fight off other information that try to occupy their place. It is like a strong, tall tree that stood up for years as we climbed it, picked its fruit, and played under its shadow. Now the tree is gone, but its shadow still remains. They will be missed.

Incomprehensible

I was introduced to Carlo Amato, the exiled prince of San Marino. He was a most charming personality, but also strict. I used to visit with him at both his estate in Nova Scotia, and at his place in Miami. One time after staying a few nights at his estate, he decided to invite a few Ministers of Nova Scotia. He was an excellent culinary professor. He had been preparing an incredible soup the night before. I still recall that day. He was standing with his help in the fancy kitchen when the doorbell rang. The butler opened the door and invited the Ministers in. I was seated in the living room doing some work. I stood up and shook hands with the Ministers, one-by-one and in French, asked them if we could serve them some drinks. The Ministers had never met Carlo, so kept referring to me as "His Excellency." Carlo was chuckling in the kitchen, especially when I said "His Excellency is cooking in the kitchen; I am only a guest." Carlo was one cool customer. He wanted to establish a scientific club, something similar to the Club of Rome for those scholars interested in doing research toward potential predictions. His estate was beautiful; a few thousand acres I believe, but the establishment of such a club would have required large sums of money to run. We had discussed the geopolitical situation and how to establish standards to make the Club of Nova Scotia a well-respected institution. It was just two days before September 11, 2001.

September 11, 2001

No building is designed to be hit by a massive airplane, and most certainly no airplane is designed to take such an impact. An airplane will even go down after being hit by Canadian Geese. It is recorded that during cavalry charges, the horses manage to miss each other and pass asymptotically to each other. Yet somehow, it is only the human mind that is twisted with so much hatred that blowing oneself to pieces, just to kill someone else is acceptable.

It might be a point of interest to compare the transmission of neurobiological information to electromagnetic wave communication. Guided drones would not have a problem with destroying themselves; they do not need a cause, as humans seem to. I want to ask my species to imagine the treatment that we give animals. What if someday they were to justify the cause of getting rid of us, once and for all? After all there is a big difference between being politically upset, which some people are, compared to the situation of animals, where their children are slaughtered, skinned, cooked, and eaten. That is what should bring out madness in any species. But for humans, to claim that they are mad is foolish, as they have language, a tongue, and the power to show the injustices done to them, even if they have to walk by the White House or any other national buildings in their country in protest. Following a "policy of madness" will result in tyranny. Tyranny has a short lifespan with a very large collateral damage done to the mostly innocent population. We should be reminded of the second law of thermodynamics: each time a process of reconstruction is repeated, it is never the same and energy is lost forever, even if it is in the form of heat. Each time we destroy and rebuild, we have less energy available to do other things. Entropy and an increase in disorder are equivalent and will rule.

If anger management has any meaning, then it should be based on the fact that there are no short cuts in the ups and downs of life. Screaming, yelling, and even breaking dishes is okay. By the way, I haven't done the latter. I should really try it, just for the hell of it. Releasing the pressure is so natural that all over the cosmos, stars, and planets under pressure do it. Keeping stress within evolves into a rotten piece of one's self. One begins to look older in body and mind. For instance, in my marriage, dealing with my mother-in-law was a challenge. In short, my mother-in-law "Jenny" was a "wild stallion of the East." Her children didn't dare tell her, but by God, I did. I did it in the form of teasing and kicks but not viciously, because I actually liked her, even though she may have seen it differently. I kept one hell of a poker face which, by itself, was fun. Perhaps every son-in-law should try it. Jenny would fight with Luba and ask me to take her side. My advice to humanity is to not ever do that.

One day we walked into a new doctor's office. He didn't know who the patient was. He approached me, shook my hand, and innocently asked me, "are you allergic to anything?" I spontaneously answered, "Yes, to my mother-in-law." The three of us and the two nurses laughed. Another time, we were on vacation with my mother-in-law (hint here; think first before you do that!). It was late in the afternoon in August and I was lost. I believe I was somewhere in the South. I had a small white Honda with an escargot roof rack, which made the whole car look like a small space capsule. No one should ever depend on my knowledge of direction. When God was distributing directional know-how, I must have been absent. Here we were in a two-lane road in the Deep South. A state trooper stopped my car. He came and looked inside the car, packed with five people—Luba, Christopher, Natalie, Jenny and me. I knew what he was thinking: how in the hell can you pack a small car with so many people and a roof rack full of things? He was a good size himself and could not have fit in my car, even if it had been only the two of us. I got out of the car and, just about the same time, another sheriff's car stopped in front of his. We were now three cars in a row. All four officers and I were standing and exchanging information. The road had barely any cars driving on it. The state trooper said, "You were driving over the speed limit. I have to write you a summons of $100 dollars. Would you like to pay now or drive with me to the station?" I responded, "Officer, please add another $150 to my summons and take my mother-in-law with you." That was it; the four officers started in with their own mother-in-law anecdotes. The State Trooper decided not to issue a ticket. Luba asked me, "What was going on?" I drove away saluting my newly-found friends and laughingly said, "Man, I almost sold your mother." Natalie asked, "How much for, Dad?" Chris picked up and answered, "twenty-nine dollars." Luba exclaimed, "That's enough kids." Even Jenny had a smile on her face, which was rare, believe you me, but as they say, c'est la vie. You can either laugh it off or drive yourself crazy.

Culture

The family was growing. Henry and Laura had four children: Cameron, Claire, Kimberly, and Christine. Luba's brother Vladimir and his wife Scarlet had two children: Nicole and Michael. Luba's sister Nadia and her husband Bob had three children: Brendon, Bryan, and Danielle. Christopher, Natalie, and Dimitri had more cousins than I. But having a family doesn't always mean a smooth ride. Just getting or having a picture taken was a battle. Bob, Henry, and I used to say this is why the Assyrians lost their empire, because they argue about just everything. "Is the sky blue? No! I have seen it to be black." The kids would laugh seeing grown-ups being silly. There was no point to it. People argued just to be heard. It was like being in New York City. People talk loudly to be noticed. But culture is just that—it is something like an addiction. One could go through withdrawals without it and could overdose with it. The bonding is based on memory and senses. One may remember the food or may like the music. One may like the social gatherings or simply the drinking. One feels fitted. Cultures have a fabric, and each culture carries its own colorful base. Culture is a background, like space and time. It is only there to describe a social existence. On its own, it cannot exist. Without it, society does not exist. Society is like a field that permeates its background, its culture.

Our family members permeate our culture for a few more generations. But at the end, the Assyrians will remain only part of the collection in various museums and finally dissipate into the memory of wider space. Someday, somewhere, an archeologist will search and find a shadow where once stood a strong tree. Actually, in Hebrew "Ashur" means "strong tree."

Joy and Sadness

On Easter day of 2006, I had a major surgery. Doctors removed 10 centimeters in diameter of my liver and my gallbladder. Both were infected. Christopher was graduating from Cornell University at the time, and I was unable to attend his graduation. This was very upsetting. The doctors told me that at least I was alive, since my chances of pulling through were very slim.

Natalie was in her senior year studying at The American University in Washington, D.C. I was thankful that both of my children were progressing well. A few months had passed. One evening I got a call from Henry. He was waiting for me at our house. As I walked into the house, he and Luba were in the kitchen and told me to sit down because they had bad news. Ivan had passed away in Paris where he and his fiancé were to be married the next day. He was 73. They had flown from California for their wedding, and he returned in a coffin. Ivan was buried a few graves away from my parents. A few months later, Vladimir, Luba's brother, was diagnosed with lung cancer and died within three months. Some people say bad news comes in threes. Either way, it was much harder for those who had to face the loss of their loved ones day in and day out.

Christopher met Jenny Ho at Cornell University and they were married by 2009. Luba and I had our first grandchild on September 21, 2013, Theodor Atour Kakovitch-Ho. His name was longer than he was at his birth. He was and is a joy; energetic, handsome, and smart. Statistically speaking, Theo added another 0.000000038% to China's population. One day, at the age of three, we were talking and he spontaneously said, "Nana I am Chinese." Luba and I started laughing. I asked, "Theo, what is Chinese?" He responded very clearly, "Chinese is my family in Chicago." He was right. If only politicians were able to realize that we are all one family, living in different cities.

Vigilance

For every one of us who has ever lived, there are millions upon millions of brothers and sisters who were denied their existence. During a conception, millions upon millions of sperm are headed towards an egg. Only a few make it (in most cases it's one and only one) and we are born. Whether we know it or not, we end up being the champions that nature chose. The human genome is beginning to give some answers, but not with respect to "information," only with codes at the molecular scale. Somehow, there was information adjusting physiology for its future. For instance, eyes must be developed even though there is no need for a pair of eyes inside a dark and fluid-filled womb. The eyes are needed not for the womb, but for the future.

Millenniums passed and we evolved to communicate and build tools. Our brain is wired no differently than hardware awaiting more and more advanced software and apps to be inserted. We eventually comprehended each other's communication and built a fragile living web. The human civilization was born.

We have weapons such as the USS Kentucky (SSBN-7370), the United States Navy Ohio-Class ballistic-missile submarine, whose 11 missiles have the power to destroy a continent. And this is only one submarine of many in the arsenal of the U.S. Navy. Imagine what others may have and how many are needed to kill us three times over. Remember that nature isn't finished with us just yet. No need to push our luck; darker days are also part of life. History is unquestionable witness to that. Science pointed us toward nature's tenacity. We may just experience its true ferocity.

Out-of-the-Box Thinking

I established a good friendship with a team, which we later referred to as "La Mad," from the name of a restaurant in Reston, Virginia, "la Madeleine." The team consisted of basically computer wizards, not exactly nerds, but not too far from it either. In our meetings, which were mostly on Fridays, we covered all that could be covered in few hours. Someone recording us would certainly go crazy. But that was just the fun of it all—carefree, at least for few hours. However, these were learned people and true scientists, like Russ Vane, John Bodnar, Dave Lambert, Tim Donohue, Bret Berlin, John Horowitz, Doug Samuelson, and Sabine O'Hara, to mention few. My other team was "Clearton," consisting of three professors of computer science, Byunggu Yu, Junwhan Kim, Dong H. Jeong, and of course Sabine O'Hara. Our team covered subjects from neural-networking to finance. Also, there were the K.I Industries, LLC, where my friends Bill McGrath and Jeff Cowan were always busy getting involved with another venture, which at times turned into an adventure.

One interesting aspect of thinking outside the box, to quote my friend Sabine O'Hara, is "that one dares to question the answers and not just answer the questions." It appeared to me that all I encountered seemed to be a solution already solved by nature. We may not be able to ignite a fusion as of yet, but every star that exists or ever existed has resolved the physics of nuclear fusion. Every plant has figured out how to extract energy out of electromagnetic radiation. Every cell has come up with a method for how to divide and propagate itself. My universe appears to be a cosmos of answers, but what is the question? I stand as an answer to what? To an imperfect entity, imprisoned for a short time by the gravity of a massive rock, in orbit around a faraway star of a distant galaxy? To search in the darkness for "dark matter" and "dark energy?" Am I a momentary remembrance of a deeper past?

I seem to be lost in a forest that has no trees. I look for water in a desert that is dry. I dream in a realm where no one sleeps. I am

In the Name of Life

organized order in the midst of chaos. Is it I, or is it nature itself that is forgetful? I recognize the sadness of a frail and confused cosmos in expansion, with many questions remaining. Nature is wishing that a speck such as I would journey into isolated spaces, to permeate like a field, the inner layers of her memory. A field that resembles nothing that humans have ever encountered in the physical realm, but of pure mathematics and functions. She is in search of a force. A force that never changed—invariant, non-directional, scalar, reigned since the beginning of time during the big bang, when she was so young. A force that shared the gene of its siblings—the Newtonian force of gravity, or the Coulomb force in electronics. She is a force that still interacts with all events but remains unchanged and determined for the cosmos's stability to be retained.

We were able to turn Newton's or Coulomb's forces into tangible applications and technologies. Our engines were basically combustion engines, including jet or rocket engines. Our understanding of the concept of energy followed a path from kinetic energy to Einstein's famous mass-energy equivalence. In quantum, the concept of energy relates to the product of the angular momentum and the frequency. Even though, at first, these two concepts appear different, the fact is that they are members of the same family, viewed from a dimensional-analysis perspective. Nature never meant to complicate things, it was our brain that did. A more generalized form of energy, of the same family as the previous ones, is the product of angular momentum and vorticity. Vorticity has the same dimensions of frequency but is not of the electromagnetic family. Vorticity is based on natural restrictions. Everyone on an aircraft carrier knows that the length of the runway is limited, whereas the aircrafts have variable speeds. The ratio of an aircraft's velocity to the runway's length is what a vorticity is. It is the ratios of velocities to limited distances. In the fancy language of mathematics, we call one such operation as the rotation of a velocity field "CURL." In the cosmos, the speed with which the universe could expand is limited to its three-dimensional space variation. The primordial force, "the fifth force," is predicted to be a function of vorticity.

Contraction and expansion are two important principles at work in nature. Imagine if we were able to have contraction and expansion taking place at the same time, but not at the same rate. What kind of an engine could we have then? At the cosmic scale, dark energy expands our universe and gravity contracts matter within it. But, so far, we don't understand the entanglement between the two. For the sake of thinking out-of-the-box, if some day, in futuristic space travels, one could expand space-time in front of a vehicle, and contract it in the back of it, then the vehicle would act as a space-time bubble. There is nothing in physics that says space-time bubbles cannot move faster than light. However, as we are still in our age of technology, how can we produce a simultaneous expansion-contraction engine?

I worked on the concept of using vorticities to contract and expand working fluids of higher and lower pressures. In a nutshell, this seems to be the reverse of the physics we experience. Usually, high pressure moves towards a low pressure. But the reverse occurs when a large amount of lower-pressure is pulled into an area of higher-pressure. A Venturi system generates a small amount of low pressure by increasing the velocity of a fluid through a narrow gap. But it is limited in its performance. This is because a Venturi works based on the Bernoulli's principle, which is a special case of vorticity studies. Energy can be extracted from the angular momentum and vorticity of the fluid. This patented system was copyrighted as "Flo-Vex." Flo-Vex has many fields of use. The system could extract additional energy from a wasted and dispatched energy. I formed Kakovitch Industries, LLC, and with my friends William McGrath, Jeffrey Cowan, and the professional consultation of Sabine O'Hara in the field of agriculture, we excelled in the field of Urban Aquaculture Technology. Kakovitch Industries designs, manufactures, and installs aquaponics and hydroponics systems in urban areas.

Flo-Vex was proof of a concept that came from an understanding of works that look different from our everyday experiences. Contraction and expansion seem to be opposite to one another. Yet they are two different sides of the same coin. What happens when a coin is in spin? Both sides coexist in the same system. When we develop tangible applications to such coexistences, we are thinking out-of-the-box.

I have been asked to see if we can deter or stop a hurricane. The eye of the hurricane creates low pressure based on vortex. Flo-Vex has been able to generate space vacuum. One can use nature against nature to fight a hurricane's low pressure—we can use Flo-Vex's even lower pressure. We have to be able to pierce the wall of the eye. This is like putting a bullet through the window of an airplane—lowest pressure always wins. Hurricanes cause billions of dollars in damage and devastation and human misery. We must and possibly can stop hurricanes. After all, we live in the 21st century.

Final Stage

I have reached my 77th birthday. Luba is 74, Christopher and Jenny are 33, and Natalie is 30. My first granddaughter, Nora, was born on July 13th, 2017. My sister Rita is 87 years old. I am in my car on the way to visit her. I didn't know whether it was my fault or the lady's in the other car, but either way, she gave me the finger. Oh well, there is still someone who considers me sexy. I've been through worse. Thank you, anyway.

We all have experienced the effect of wanting to remember something and feeling as though "it is just on the tip of my tongue," yet we lose it in the ocean of other information flying by. We concentrate and try to remember it, but it is just not there, as if memories, like space, also expand and rearrange themselves through a "phase transition" and dissipate into a thinner and thinner layer of what was once us. But the expansion of space is described as due to an unknown energy, or "dark energy." Could this kind of rearrangement form a "dark memory?" Are memories dissipated, or are they being rearranged? At times, we move through our lives daydreaming about a future that is no longer there. I heard a car crash. It was the lady who had passed me earlier. She had slammed into another car. I stopped my car, as it looked extremely bad. People gathered, and then came the emergency vehicles. What hopes was she carrying with her? Where was she in her thoughts? Did she ever imagine that this was going to be the end of her life's road? We are all on a razor's edge of stability—any slippage and we are done for. We are well aware that even the stars in our galaxy die, but it is hard to be a statistic. There should be a signpost based on mathematical "sequencing," showing that humanity, minus any one of us, has its own meaning and signature, different from all others. If not remembered by us, it should at least be recorded somewhere in the cosmos. If energy and information are both conserved, then how is it possible to be forgotten?

In the Name of Life

Is death a humbling reality, or are there loopholes in the second law of thermodynamics? The answer is yes, there are loopholes, but energy must be added from the outside to rearrange information. Then a new "phase transition" takes over. Perhaps one could theoretically live much longer. But would you like to live with an incurable disease for 1,000 years? Or would you be pissed off if you thought you were going to live for 1,000 years and someone kills you when you are only 20? Who is the person who thinks about eternity? Doesn't he or she realize that, humbly stated, we are finite and don't owe the universe? The rate of creation in a short time is greater than the rate of the decay in an infinite time.

I don't believe that life is, or ever has been, a foolish game. Every conversation does not concern itself with only us, and nothing else at all. There is no emptiness beyond us. And in all sincerity, we are not the only thing left on the stage to end the play.

I might have understood the meaning of my life, or I might not have. I am just fine with the outcome. I have had a fantastic family, friends of all nationalities, faiths, education, and professions, and children and grandchildren. I like the spirituality of music, the facts of science, and the freedom of the human soul. I am a devout Christian, Muslim, and Jew, and so what? Abraham himself did not get it right. So what if the big bang is a "white elephant" and time is of a weird dimension. Let time be a holographic projection of ourselves backwards and frontwards. Further from the projection, there is less information, and closer, more information. Go as far as you want, go where there is no information, no beginning, no big bang, and no time. Perhaps you will find God being bored, sitting and doing nothing. Or you may just discover that your future is just as relevant to your present as your past.

But for crying out loud, think a bit about it; "you only know, what you can measure." The amount of information from the past until now, available in the 13.8 billion years of history of this universe, is something like $10^{10^{123}}$, whereas the maximum "measurable" value is $10^{10^{90}}$. There is an incredible amount of information that is impossible to know. So, for God's sake, don't go and kill people for what they don't know, or for what they may not agree with you about. No one person can be a know-it-all, and no matter what, we are one species of the same family. As my grandson, Theo, sees it, his Chinese family lives in Chicago, and his Assyrian family lives in Virginia. We are all one, living in different cities.

My sister Rita, my second mother, my godmother, has had dementia for a few years now. Henry and Laura have her and Henry (father) with them in Vienna, Virginia, just few miles away from our house. I drove out to visit my sister recently. She regresses into a younger and younger age in her mind. She looks at me but does not recognize me. I have dissipated in her mind. I don't know if I even exist in her mind anymore. I sit, and through her eyes, go back into the past. Once she was young and strong. And now, in the midst of an increasing disorder, she is a frail and confused expansion, no different than the cosmos, with still many questions. I look deep into her eyes and smile. She smiles back. She does not recognize her only child, Henry. We both sit like two shadows from the past in interaction with one another, to recollect that we also existed once. Thank God, we are still mortal.

Farewell my loved ones, farewell.

www.ingramcontent.com/pod-product-compliance
Lightning Source LLC
Chambersburg PA
CBHW071716090426
42738CB00009B/1788